W9-BSC-788

Rather Die Than Live - Jonah

William M. Pickard

EDUCATION AND CULTIVATION DIVISION
BOARD OF GLOBAL MINISTRIES, THE UNITED METHODIST CHURCH
475 RIVERSIDE DRIVE, NEW YORK, NEW YORK 10027

Copyright © 1974, William M. Pickard
All rights reserved.
Printed in the United States of America.

Library of Congress Cataloging

Pickard, William M.   1921-
  Rather die than live—Jonah.

  Bibliography: p.
  1. Bible. O.T. Jonah—Study—Text-books.
I. Title.
BS1605.5.P52   224'.92'007   74-4352

The Scripture quotations in this publication, except where specifically noted, are from the Revised
Standard Version of the Bible, copyright 1946 and
1952, by the Division of Christian Education, National Council of the Churches of Christ in the USA.

So once upon a very present time,
maybe today, tomorrow, yesterday,
the Word of Yahweh comes to Johnny Jonah,
the son of Amittai or Mr. Jones:
"Arise—this is to say, get off your duff,
your cozy status in Jerusalem,
and get yourself to Nineveh, the place,
it's any place, where life is less than life,
men less than men, where light is turned to dark,
joy into mourning, peace to bloody war,
where ways of death absorb the wealth and mind
of all the living.*

* From B. Davie Napier, *Time of Burning* (Philadelphia: Pilgrim Press, 1970), p. 79. Copyright © 1970 United Church Press. Used by permission.

to
MARY ANN
whose love enables
me to live

CONTENTS
THE STUDY

STUDENT AND TEACHER AIDS

PREFACE

We were having a School of Missions at Knox Church in Manila. I decided to preach a series of sermons on the book of *Jonah*. Looking for materials I was amazed at how little has been written on *Jonah* in recent years. From the perspective of ten years on the mission field, the book began speaking to me in a new way. I mulled over it for more than a month.

Then one day it happened. As I was crossing Manila Bay late one Saturday afternoon, I sat in the stern of the boat enthralled by the grandeur of the open sea set ablaze with a magnificent tropical sunset. Jonah was far from my mind. But suddenly he seemed to come aboard, and the entire drama, portrayed so poignantly in the pages of the Old Testament, flashed before me. Verses began leaping at me with startling vigor. Every verse seemed to speak to a particular contemporary issue. I hurriedly scribbled some notes. Much research and study has gone into this book since that Saturday afternoon, but the central core of its message was received on Manila Bay as *Jonah* spoke to me.

The pages that follow, then, are simply an attempt to allow *Jonah* to speak to our generation. As *Jonah* has spoken to me, I have stood both condemned and challenged. I have marveled at the depth and the breadth of the author's insight and the daring with which he proclaimed God's judgment on his own generation. I have therefore not hesitated to make a bold and imaginative application of the book to the current scene. *Jonah* has many facets both reflecting and also sending piercing rays of light into our modern dilemmas.

The issues discussed here are life and death issues. There will therefore be differences of opinion on many of them, for important questions always have many facets. The reader will want to challenge the writer at times and to debate with him. The writer encourages this, for knowing his own fallibility, he makes no claim other than that of a sincere and serious attempt to grapple with the contemporary crisis in the light of God's word as it comes to us through *Jonah*. If the book will stimulate others to grapple with these issues, the writer dares to believe that God may use it in the churches to augment the movement already under way in our day toward a deeper spirituality and broader social concern. He trusts that it may stimulate serious discussion and action as the church moves in new and ever challenging areas of mission in the 1970's.

Writing this book has been a deeply emotional experience for me. C. H. Cornill said that though he had read *Jonah* at least a hundred times, he could not pick it up or even speak of it without tears rising in his eyes and his pulse beating faster. Tears have often filled my eyes also. The book overwhelms one with the breadth and depth of God's love in contrast to the tragic suffering that results from the senseless denial of this love in our world. The writer therefore confesses freely that he is writing for a verdict, not for entertainment or mere discussion. He does this without the slightest hesitation because he is profoundly convinced of the power of Christ to transform all persons and to liberate all of us from the terrible bondage of attitudes and systems that enslave and threaten to destroy us.

Writing a book is always a corporate venture. It is impossible for me to acknowledge my debt to all who have contributed in one way or another. However, I must mention several persons without whom the work would have been impossible. First, to my wife, Mary Ann, I owe a debt that can never be fully acknowledged. She has contributed so much that she should be listed as co-author. In addition she has typed and retyped draft after draft, always patient and efficient.

Second, I am deeply indebted to a wonderful group of women in Montgomery, Alabama, who have read the manuscript, met with me regularly for discussion and suggestions and have been largely responsible for Student and Teacher Aids. They are: Mary Ellen Bullard, Martha Watson, Mary S. Stevens, Susie Peach Foster, Gwen Pearson and Kate Lindsey. In addition to this group, Rev. Frank Arnold of the Dexter Avenue United Methodist Church in downtown Montgomery afforded me the opportunity of testing the study in a local church setting as a part of the church's annual lecture series.

Several colleagues in the Philippines and the United States have been gracious enough to read the manuscript or portions of it and have made many valuable suggestions: Rev. Joseph Bogle, Dr. Gerald Anderson, Rev. Hugh Lormor, the late Bishop Costen J. Harrell, Dr. George S. Tarry, Dr. Barnes Tatum, Dr. George Landes, Boone Bowen and the late Dr. E. Stanley Jones. To them I express my heartfelt thanks. Though the book is much richer for all of these various contributions, the writer alone assumes full responsibility for its contents and for whatever defects it may have.

To the wonderful people of my own congregation, the Woodland United Methodist Church, I also want to express sincere appreciation. They sustain in fellowship, support in love and stimulate in mutual discussion even when—or most especially when—we see issues, even emotion-packed issues, from quite different perspectives. This caring and sharing fellowship is what the church should be as we all seek to bring our lives more and more under the control of Christ in an ever enlarging fellowship that embraces all persons in God's Kingdom.

Finally, to my students at Huntingdon College and to my own children I want to say a word of deep gratitude. Their searching questions and critical judgments have inspired me to examine afresh my own understanding of the Christian faith in today's fast changing world. Because of them I have been able to discern (and in this book have dared to confess) that in many ways my own generation has been a Jonah generation, too sure that we have had the answers and thus wanting to insist on our own way. I have learned that hearing God's word may mean change at those places where it is hardest to change, and even change at those places where we have been convinced that we do not need to change.

THE STUDY

WORD

Now the word of the LORD came to Jonah. . . .

—Jonah 1:1.

Jonah and the Whale

A modern painting depicting the story of Jonah bears the following inscription in bold letters:

Jonah, fleeing from the fulfillment of God's command was ship-wrecked, cast into the sea and swallowed by a great fish. At length, spewn up on the shore he carried out his mission. Men cannot be contented running from God. He has made us for Himself, and we can only find true happiness living according to His commands.[1]

This nutshell description of the message of *Jonah* is quite common, but the amazing thing is that it misses two of the most important facts of the book: Jonah did not intentionally carry out God's mission, and certainly he did not find peace and happiness. The book closes with Jonah so unhappy he wants to die.

Jonah is one of the best known and yet at the same time, one of the least known books of the entire Bible. Almost everyone thinks that he or she knows one fact about *Jonah:* that Jonah was swallowed by a whale. But even this information is not entirely correct. The book of *Jonah* does not mention a whale. The word *whale* comes into the story from an incorrect translation of the Greek word κῆτος in Matthew 12:40 in the King James Version. (For some reason the error is repeated in the Revised Standard Version.) Κῆτος is the name of a genus or class of fish that may include seals, dolphins, sharks, whales and other large sea animals. The correct translation is reflected in the New English Bible where the word in Matthew 12:40 is rendered "sea-monster." The Hebrew expression used in the text of *Jonah* means "large fish." God prepared a special fish, according to the text, to swallow Jonah, and there is no indication that this fish was a whale. However, people still talk about "Jonah and the whale"—and here their knowledge of the book ends.

The whale motif has so distorted the book of *Jonah* that the true message of the prophet has seldom been heard. For the frivolous, the story is the "granddaddy of all fishermen's lies." For the superstitious the term *Jonah* is a synonym for bad luck. A person who gets all the bad breaks may begin to feel that he is a "Jonah," and when misfortune strikes a group, one is sure to hear the question, "Who is the 'Jonah' among us?" The great Old Testament scholar, George Adam Smith, said, "And this is the tragedy of the Book of Jonah, that a book which is made the means of one of the most sublime revelations of truth in the Old Testament should be known to most only for its connection with a whale." [2]

It is indeed a tragedy, for the book has a tremendous message which our age needs desperately to hear. C. H. Cornill describes *Jonah* as one of the "deepest and grandest things ever written" and advises one approaching the book to "Take off thy shoes, for the place whereon thou standest is holy ground." [3] Bishop Costen J. Harrell considers the book the climax of the entire prophetic movement in Israel. He says that "with the proclamation of these unchanging truths [of Jonah] the prophetic canon ends." [4] George Adam Smith points out that it is in *Jonah* that the truth expressed in *Acts* 11:18, "Then to the Gentiles also God has granted repentance unto life" received its fullest expression anywhere in the Old Testament. [5] Charles Reade, author of *The Cloister and the Hearth,* a book considered by some to be the greatest historical novel in the English language, writes: "Jonah is the most beautiful story ever written in so small a compass. It contains 48 verses, 1,328 English words. One does not get far in an English novel in 1,328 words. There is growth of character, a distinct plot worked out without haste or crudity. Only a great artist could have hit on a perfect proportion between dialogue and narrative." [6] George L. Robinson says that "the book of *Jonah* strikes the high-water mark of Old Testament theology," and that it is "the noblest, broadest, and the most Christian of all Old Testament Literature." [7] Thus, the book of *Jonah*, which in many ways stands closer to the New Testament than any other book of the Old Testament, surely demands a fair hearing.

Jonah and Israel

The book of *Jonah* may have been written sometime between 500 B.C. and 300 B.C.[8] It is a story about a Hebrew prophet who lived three to four hundred years earlier—around 800-750 B.C. If this dating is correct, it means two things: first, the author of the book was not the historical Jonah, but an unnamed Hebrew prophet who wrote about Jonah. The reader may wish to go into this question in more detail. A summary of the factors involved in determining the authorship and date of the book is included in an appendix found on page 123.

Second, the dating of *Jonah* just after 500 B.C. means that the setting for the message of the book is post-exilic Israel. If we are to understand the message of *Jonah* for our day, we must first understand its message for the day in which it was written. Therefore, we will take a brief look at Israel around 500 B.C.

Approximately 1020 B.C., the first Kingdom in Israel had been established under the leadership of Saul. Saul's successor, David (1000-961 B.C.), built a strong kingdom, expanded its borders and brought great glory to Israel. The Jewish people ever after looked to the reign of David as the "Golden Age" of their national history. David's son, Solomon, however, was a spendthrift. He built a magnificent palace and a magnificent temple. He maintained a harem of 700 wives and 300 mistresses, and in general adopted the style of an extravagant potentate. He placed heavy taxes on the people to support this opulence, and when he died (approximately 922 B.C.) there was a revolt. A number of other factors were also involved in the split such as tribal rivalries and geographical, economic and ideological differences. The kingdom which had lasted for about one hundred years split into the Northern Kingdom called Israel, with its capital at Shechem, and the southern kingdom called Judah with its capital at Jerusalem.

These kingdoms had an up and down existence for two hundred years. In 721 B.C. the Assyrians conquered and destroyed the Northern Kingdom. The Southern Kingdom, Judah, lasted another hundred and thirty-five years down to 586 B.C.[9]

Jonah lived in the Northern Kingdom during the reign of Jeroboam II (786-746 B.C.). This made him a contemporary of Amos of Tekoa. The only place in the Old Testament outside the book of *Jonah* where the prophet Jonah is mentioned is in II Kings 14:25: "He [Jeroboam II] restored the border of Israel from the entrance of Hamath as far as the Sea of the Arabah, according to the word of the Lord, the God of Israel, which he spoke by his servant Jonah the son of Amittai, the prophet, who was from Gath-hepher." This verse gives us three items of information about Jonah. First, he was the son of Amittai. Second, he was from Gath-Hepher (the modern el Meshhed), a village in Zebulon (later Galilee) about three miles north of Nazareth (see *Joshua* 19:10-13). One of the many Muslim tombs of Nebi Yunas (Prophet Jonah) is at el Meshhed, and both Christians and Muslims accept this as his home place. There is also a Jonah tomb at the "Nebi Yunas Mound," one of the two mounds that comprise the ancient site of Nineveh, and some believe Jonah was buried there. A glance at a map of ancient Palestine will show that Gath-hepher was along the much traveled caravan route between Egypt and Mesopotamia. Jonah would therefore have had ample opportunity to know about events in Syria and to have traveled as far as Nineveh.

The third item of information given in *II Kings* 14:25 concerning Jonah is that he was a highly nationalistic prophet. His major activity (at least that activity which the historian records) was connected with the military victory that expanded the borders of the kingdom under Jeroboam II and brought great glory to Israel. This prophecy gave him the reputation of being an extreme nationalist, and his name was later associated with that narrow kind of patriotism that so easily degenerates into bigotry and that reached such extreme proportions in Israel immediately following the exile. Because he was an extreme nationalist, it is not surprising that he would harbor deep feelings of hatred for Israel's oppressors, chief among which was Assyria. Conjecture says he could have been present in 721 B.C. when the final carnage took place that resulted in the destruction of Israel. At any rate, he experienced both the glory of Israel's victories under Jeroboam's reign and also the cruel atrocities of the Assyrians. Jacques Ellul says that the Assyrians were the "most cruel people of antiquity. [Nineveh] scorched its enemies alive to decorate its walls and pyramids with their skins." [10] So hatred for Nineveh, capital of Assyria, though not to be defended, is entirely understandable.

In 586 B.C. the Babylonians, who had by this time defeated the Assyrians, conquered the Southern Kingdom, Judah. Jerusalem was razed, the temple destroyed and the people carried off to Babylon as captives. The next fifty years are spoken of as the Babylonian captivity or the exile. In 538 B.C. Babylon fell to the Persians. The Persian king, Cyrus, was more friendly toward the Israelites and issued a decree allowing them to return to Jerusalem. It was a time of great rejoicing. However, the effort to rebuild Jerusalem and to reestablish the Hebrew people as a nation was more difficult than expected. This is far too complex a story to go into here. But two antithetical developments that set the stage for the writing of the book of *Jonah* must be looked at in some detail.[11] They provide the key to understanding the book. The two developments were first, the growth of monotheistic universalism;[12] and second, the growth of narrow nationalistic particularism. Let us see how these two movements, each the exact opposite of the other, developed.

Monotheistic universalism developed out of the growing understanding of God among the Hebrew people. The high-water mark of Hebrew prophecy was reached just before, during and after the exile in Babylon with the appearance of *Jeremiah, II Isaiah*[13], and *Jonah*. The early pages of the Old Testament reflect the limited concept of God that many Hebrew people held in the days of Abraham, Isaac and Jacob. Expressions of monotheism as in the Yahwistic concept are found in the time of Moses, but many of the Hebrews, during the settlement in Canaan and the years of the united and divided kingdoms, seemed to have thought of Yahweh in narrow, selfish terms as a god who fought their battles for them and often demanded brutal and inhuman treatment of enemies. In Amos and the other eighth and seventh century prophets, monotheism is emphasized. However, it was the exile, calamity though it

7

was for Israel, that brought to full flower the monotheistic faith of Israel. This came about in two ways.

First, there was a reinterpretation of Israel's defeat. In the context of tribal deities, the destruction of Israel and Judah was seen as a defeat for Yahweh. Other, more powerful gods had prevailed over him—else his people would not have been defeated. As time went on, however, many of the Hebrews began to accept the view of the prophets who had seen defeat not as a sign that Yahweh had failed them, but as evidence that they had failed Yahweh. A growing sense of the universality of God led these sensitive spirits to see the exile not as a sign of Yahweh's impotence, but rather as a sign of his universal presence and power. Calamity had come to Israel, because she had been unfaithful to her covenant with Yahweh. Assyria and Babylonia were used by Yahweh as agents to carry out his punishment. If Yahweh is ruler of Assyria and Babylonia, it is only one step further to the claim that he is ruler of all and that he is in fact the only God who really is; others are mere idols. First Isaiah insisted that there is but one God and that he rules the entire world. He is the God of all. He uses kings and empires for his purposes. *Isaiah* 10:5 says "Ah, Assyria, the rod of my anger, the staff of my fury!" Assyria is God's instrument, God's rod. But Assyria is haughty and ruthless; so Isaiah says that God "will punish the arrogant boasting of the king of Assyria and his haughty pride" (10:12). Second Isaiah says, "I am the Lord, and there is no other, besides me there is no God" (45:5).

The second way in which the exile gave rise to a monotheistic view was that there developed a new realization of Yahweh's presence in the strange, faraway land of Babylon. When the Hebrews were first carried off into captivity, they bemoaned their fate: "By the waters of Babylon, there we sat down and wept . . . How shall we sing the Lord's song in a foreign land?" (*Psalms* 137:1, 4). But to their surprise some of them discovered that God was no less present in Babylon than in Jerusalem. His universal presence meant that they could never be away from him. One great spirit declared:

Whither shall I go from thy Spirit?
    Or whither shall I flee from thy presence?
If I ascend to heaven, thou art there!

8

If I make my bed in Sheol, thou art there!
If I take the wings of the morning
  and dwell in the uttermost parts of the sea,
even there thy hand shall lead me,
  and thy right hand shall hold me. (*Psalms* 139:7-10)

This universalism was more than mere monotheism. Thanks to the rich heritage of the Old Testament prophets it was an ethical monotheism. The covenant between Yahweh and Israel, which had originally been quite narrowly conceived by Israel, now came to take on worldwide dimensions. The new sense of Yahweh's universality led many Israelites to begin to see themselves in a new light. No longer were they to think of themselves as a favored few who would enjoy a special relationship to Yahweh, but rather as ambassadors of light and love to all.

Unfortunately, however, the exile had exactly the opposite effect on many Hebrews. Whereas for some the vision of God was enlarged, for others it was narrowed. For the first group the exile pointed in the direction of universalism. For the second group it pointed in the direction of exclusivism. This latter group believed that all of Israel's troubles were due to the heathen influences that had been allowed to creep into Jewish life. They, therefore, considered that the solution was to purge all of these corrupting elements and, in this way, reestablish the covenant with Yahweh. In their zeal they decreed a complete segregation from all non-Israelitish people and placed a ban on everything foreign. They forbade all mixed marriages (*Nehemiah* 13:23-27), and Ezra even went so far as to command that all the Israelites who had married foreign wives divorce them. *Ezra*, chapter 10, records how an assembly was called to see that the decree was carried out. The measures were directed especially against the Samaritans, who were considered a half-breed people since they were the descendants of the Israelites and the other peoples who remained in the area of the Northern Kingdom after its fall in 721 B.C.

One can readily see how this approach to the reestablishment of the covenant, however sincere it might have been, quickly developed into smugness and bigotry. The covenant soon became synonymous with racial exclusiveness. Thus in contrast to the greatheartedness of II Isaiah there arose the

9

narrowmindedness expressed so forcefully in the books of *Nahum, Ezra* and *Nehemiah*. Furthermore, it is quite easy to see how many of the Israelites would have been so deeply embittered by the exile that a "hate the enemy" approach would readily appeal to them. To the unspeakable atrocities the people had suffered for many years, the exile added humiliation. Forced into a state of vassalage by the Assyrians and ultimately taken into captivity by the Babylonians, the Israelites suffered a severe blow to their pride as God's chosen people. Deeply embittered, many of them came to be possessed by one dream, one passionate hope that God would one day vindicate them by utterly destroying their accursed enemies, and in so doing prove that he was more powerful than the gods of the other nations.

This narrow, vengeful spirit found full expression in the books of *Nahum, Ezra, Nehemiah, Daniel* and *Esther*. Note how *Nahum* alters *Exodus* 34:6, used by the author of *Jonah* to express the love of God (*Jonah* 4:2), and combines it with verse 7 in such a way that it depicts a god of vengeance: "The Lord is slow to anger and of great might, and the Lord will by no means clear the guilty" (*Nahum* 1:3). The phrase "abounding in steadfast love" is changed to "of great might," for Nahum did not want to speak of love in connection with Israel's enemies. The expression from *Exodus* 34:7, "will by no means clear the guilty," is used by Nahum as a justification for vengeance. Nahum exults over the fall of Nineveh: "All who hear the news of you clap their hands over you" (3:19). Read all of the short book of *Nahum*, which pictures the God of Israel as one who wreaks vengeance on his adversaries. Because the Gentiles had persecuted God's chosen people, the fiercest wrath of God would speedily descend upon them. God had now brought his chosen out of exile; his next step would be to punish the wicked heathen with utter destruction.

The writers of *Ruth*,[14] *Jonah* and *II Isaiah*, in the spirit of the universalism described above, felt called to challenge this narrow vengeful attitude. To those enamored of Ezra's emphasis on reestablishing the covenant, the book of *Jonah* says:

Yes, reestablish the covenant by all means, but remember that the covenant also makes clear that "the LORD, the

10

LORD, [is] a God merciful and gracious, slow to anger, and abounding in steadfast love and faithfulness, keeping steadfast love for thousands, forgiving iniquity and transgression and sin. . . ." (*Exodus* 34:6b-7a, paraphrased in *Jonah* 4:2)[15]

Israel had always insisted that because of the special covenant relationship, this passage applied to it only. Gentiles were excluded from the steadfast love and forgiveness. However, II Isaiah boldly applied the covenant to all peoples, calling upon Israel to be a "light to the nations": "I am the Lord, I have called you in righteousness, I have taken you by the hand and kept you; I have given you as a covenant to the people, a light to the nations . . ." (*Isaiah* 42:6). "I will give you as a light to the nations that my salvation may reach to the end of the earth" (*Isaiah* 49:6). See also *Isaiah* 52:15; 56:1-8; 60:3 and 66:18-23. All of these passages look for the salvation of the nations through Israel. Israel was chosen for this specific purpose, according to Isaiah, and the author of *Jonah* uses the verse from *Exodus* in order to make it abundantly clear that God's covenant love extends to all people.

Moreover, there had grown up in Israel a movement with a universalistic emphasis called the Wisdom Movement. Beginning probably in the tenth century B.C. during the time of Solomon, this movement came to full expression shortly before, during and after the exile. Such books as *Proverbs, Ecclesiastes,* and *Job* do not presuppose a special covenantal relationship of Yahweh with Israel, but rather presuppose a kind of universal ethic applicable to all. Job, for instance, is spoken of as man "blameless and upright, one who feared God, and turned away from evil" (*Job* 1:1). But Job was an Uzite, not a Jew. In verse 3 he is called the "greatest of all the people of the east." The writer is clearly implying a universality of God's relationship to the world and also a universal response to God. In the same way, the author of *Ruth* stresses the fact that Ruth, a Moabitess, was the great-grandmother of King David (*Ruth* 4:17).

The book of *Jonah,* then, is to be seen in the context of these two diametrically opposed views that flowered in post-exilic Israel. That they have pre-exilic roots is clear. But they came to full expression during and after the exile. Jonah is unique in that the author uses the historical Jonah, who held tenaciously to the God of Ezra, Nehemiah and Nahum, to make clear how wrong such a view of God actually is. The author shows how Jonah, holding fiercely to a narrow tribal concept of God, yet in actuality knowing full well the true character of God as a God of love and mercy, deliberately refused to proclaim God's judgment upon Nineveh for the precise reason that he feared the people would repent and be saved. And Nineveh's salvation, as is shown in the fourth chapter of *Jonah,* was the last thing Jonah desired. God rebuked Jonah, declaring that his universal love included all persons, even Ninevites. The author of the book of *Jonah* is thus speaking directly to the Israelites rebuking them for their narrow, bigoted, exclusivistic practices, and calling them to fulfill their mission to the world. There are scholars who reject this view of *Jonah,* because they see *Jonah* as basically a call to repentance rather than to mission. However, we believe it is both. The book of *Jonah* ties repentance and mission together and suggests that the call to repentance together with a changed attitude toward the Gentiles is the key to the fulfillment of Israel's mission as God's "chosen."

Jonah and the Word

The book of *Jonah,* then, had an urgent message for post-exilic Israel. It was a daring and explosive book running counter to the prevailing currents in post-exilic Jewish life. From a purely Jewish point of view it might be wondered how it ever came to be included in the Old Testament canon. The marvel of course only points up the greatheartedness of the Jewish people and the breadth and depth of the Jewish heritage. Whatever else may be said about the problem of exclusiveness in the post-exilic period, the fact that the Jewish people could include in their sacred canon such a searching critique of their own life is a mark of true greatness. Both Jews and Christians are convinced that God was at work through the prophet. The message comes through because God speaks. The marvel happens because it is God's word we are dealing with. The book of *Jonah* is far more than a simple story about an ancient prophet who had an unusual ride in the belly of a fish. It is "the word of the LORD." It is one of the great prophetic books of Israel and one of the outstanding literary masterpieces of all time. Our study should be a rich adventure.

As we begin, we need first to explore the book's literary character. Traditionally it has been looked upon as a simple historical narrative relating events in the life of an Old Testament prophet. However, careful study shows that much more is involved. Scholars have pointed to both parabolic and allegorical elements in the story that give it a deeper and richer meaning. There are differences of opinion with some scholars stressing one aspect, some another, but all three elements—history, parable and allegory—seem to be present. Jonah appears to be a story based on certain historical data, cast in a somewhat parabolic form (with exceptions noted below) and containing certain allegorical or symbolical references. Possibly a more accurate description would be to say that it is a sermon preached to Israel using facts and references with which the people were familiar. Therefore, it is hard to classify the book in any neat category. We must simply take it as it is.

Consider first that the attempt to view the book simply as a parable encounters a number of difficulties. A parable ordinarily uses fictitious, not historical characters. If we classify the book as a parable, we must then ignore the fact that its main character is an historical figure. Again, a parable ordinarily does not mention real places, such as Joppa, Tarshish and Nineveh. This principle of course is not rigid, as is seen in Jesus' parable of the Good Samaritan. But the parable, as a form of literary expression, ordinarily uses only fictitious names. Likewise, a parable is usually short, simply told, uncomplicated in plot and has one main point[16] although there may be subsidiary ones, and ordinarily does not contain allegorical references. The book of *Jonah* has a greater length and a more complicated plot than the ordinary parable. It also appears to contain certain symbolical references that introduce the element of allegory.

The attempt to classify the book as an allegory runs into trouble also. The historical character, Jonah, the real cities mentioned, together with the other elements that are foreign to the purely allegorical form of writing, make such classification inaccurate. The expansion of Israel that the historical Jonah of *II Kings* 14:25 predicted had definite relationship to both Syria and Assyria. This leads the *New Century Bible*, following S. R. Driver, to point out that "The historical Jonah had therefore a direct interest in Nineveh; and it is conceivable that he journeyed to the great city with a call of repentance from Yahweh." [17] Elijah went to Sarepta. Elisha took the word of the Lord to Damascus. Amos, though limiting his activity to Israel, thundered God's judgment upon Gaza, Tyre, Edom, Ammon, Moab and Damascus. In like manner, the historical Jonah, who as a successor to Elisha and a predecessor of Amos, was more than likely related in one way or another to Assyria, whose capital was Nineveh.

However, we must also note that the attempt to view *Jonah* as a simple historical narrative related by the prophet Jonah himself, or about the prophet, cannot do justice to the total purpose and perspective of the book. The detailed study of the message of the book that follows will seek to make this clear. Unless we see how the author uses the story of Jonah to burn, as with a branding iron, a message of great urgency into the conscience of Israel, we miss the whole purpose of the book. The story degenerates into a mere "whale's tale" at worst, or at best into a simple account of a prophet's experiences from which we may glean certain morals. Regarded in this light, the book, which was dynamite in its day and remains so in ours, is reduced to an insipid fizzle.[18]

In this writer's opinion, elements of history, parable, and allegory are present in the book of *Jonah*. This means that the conclusion of some modern scholarship that "the story is purely imaginative" [19] hardly seems warranted. It is in no sense necessary to deny the book's historical rootage in order to see its message. In fact, this historical rootage adds poignancy to the message. On the other hand, to affirm the elements of historicity in *Jonah* while denying or overlooking its basic parabolic and symbolical message is to do a gross injustice to the scripture. Since the use of history, parable and allegory in the prophetic tradition in Israel may be observed in a number of Old Testament books, the fact that the three are combined in *Jonah* should be in no way surprising.

One characteristic of ancient Israel was its realism. The people were not as given to abstract thinking as were the Greeks. Great teachings were often spelled out in story form, as is seen in the development of a whole class of literature

14

called the Haggadic Midrash. The Haggadah was inspirational and homiletical in character and was based on the story-telling technique. It was designed to make explicit, and to apply to everyday life, the great teachings of the law and the prophets. It was a method Jesus inherited. The author of *Jonah* writes in the tradition of the Haggadah. He takes an historical figure out of Israel's prophetic tradition and relates a story about him with the purpose of making explicit the universal character of God's love (see *Isaiah* 42:1-9; 49:6; 56:1-8; 60:1-3; 66:18-21). What II Isaiah teaches about the universal character of God's love, *Jonah* makes transparently clear in a story that, if grasped, burns its way into the conscience and can never be forgotten.

Jonah is the kind of story that fascinates the reader and then suddenly flips. As the plot develops the reader begins to judge and condemn the villain. Then suddenly the reader is confronted. Judgment has been declared. This was the technique used by Nathan when he faced King David (*II Samuel* 12:1-15). David had stolen Uriah's wife and then had made certain that Uriah was killed in battle. Nathan did not approach David's sin directly. Instead, he told of a rich landlord who had thousands of sheep, yet who, when he had a visitor, sent for the pet lamb of a poor tenant farmer—the only lamb the farmer had—and slew it for his guest. King David was incensed. He decreed that the rich man be put to death. Nathan then calmly replied, "You are the man." The king had condemned himself.

The story of Jonah is told in such a way that an Israelite on hearing it for the first time would assume that he or she was listening to a simple story about one of Israel's ancient prophets. As the story progressed, the listener would at first be sympathetic with Jonah. However, by the time the story neared the end, with Jonah peeved over his own minor discomfort and demanding the cruel destruction of the Ninevites—even the small children—the listener would exclaim: "Why, that is absurd! How hardhearted and callous can a person get?" Then suddenly what the story was really saying would break through the listener's consciousness. The "word of the Lord" would descend: "You are the [one]!"

The Basic Message of Jonah

Jonah is considered by this writer to be the high-water mark of Old Testament prophecy. It gathers together in one amazingly small compass the central core of Old Testament revelation of God's love. It distills out the pure essence of God's self-disclosure as the God of righteous judgment and loving mercy and, therefore, expresses the highest genius of the Hebrew heritage. As such it occupies a preeminent place in the Old Testament canon. It is one of the greatest missionary treatises ever penned. To be sure, due weight must be given to some recent Old Testament scholarship that has questioned the missionary character of *Jonah,* though it is far from convincing. These scholars have questioned whether there is a distinctly missionary message anywhere in the Old Testament. They contend that the universalism expressed in II Isaiah, *Jonah* and elsewhere in the Old Testament does not imply mission in the usual sense of this word.

Johannes Blauw, for instance, in his book, *The Missionary Nature of the Church,* maintains that we must distinguish between a centripetal and a centrifugal sense of mission in Israel. He says that we find examples of centripetal mission in the Old Testament—that is, mission in the sense of all nations being drawn to Israel. But, he insists, centrifugal mission—mission in the sense of Israel's going out to the nations—is almost nonexistent. On this basis he questions the missionary character of *Jonah.*[20]

Universalism and mission are not one and the same, and Blauw's distinction between centripetal and centrifugal mission is valid. Israel's sense of mission was, in the main, centripetal and not centrifugal. Certainly there is nothing in the Old Testament to compare with the Christian missionary movement. The Old Testament does not have a St. Paul or a "great commission" expressed in terms of *Matthew* 28:16-20. Likewise the attempt to picture Jonah as a kind of nineteenth century Christian missionary is not valid. However, it would appear that the fallacy in Blauw's position and the position of other scholars who question the missionary character of Jonah is that they define mission too narrowly. In a recent study titled *The Invitation,*[21] Hans Ruedi Weber has developed Matthew's understanding of mission. Whereas *Luke-Acts* speaks of

16

mission as "going out" (centrifugal mission) Matthew speaks of mission as "calling in" (centripetal mission). Luke sees the Christian mission as *going*. Matthew sees it as *being*. Luke in the *Acts of the Apostles* focuses on the missionary journeys of Paul. Matthew focuses on the exaltation of Christ as King, as the New Israel, and on the invitation to all nations to join in the coronation feast. Matthew and Luke complement each other. They both express the heart of Christian mission, for mission is both being and going.

Likewise, this writer would insist that the book of *Jonah* is the Old Testament precursor of the great commission that Jesus gave to the disciples, and he hopes to substantiate this view in what follows. The author of *Jonah* expresses the concept of the universal love of God on which that commission is based. Centrifugal mission can be perverted into proselytism. Centripetal mission can be perverted into pride and self-righteousness. The author of *Jonah* is challenging Israel at both points. Israel is to go out to the nations with the message of God's ethical demands, his love and his mercy (centrifugal mission), calling on them to repent and to exalt the God of justice, righteousness and love (centripetal mission). When seen in its proper light, *Jonah* contains one of the clearest missionary messages of all times. That it does not spell out mission in the Pauline sense is obvious, but the fact remains that the central theme of the book is the universal character of God's love and concern plus the clear demand for repentance, not only for Nineveh, but more particularly for Israel. And is not this the starting point of all Christian missions? Is not this the reason Christ came? "For God so loved the world . . . that whoever believes . . . ."

The missionary message, then, is inherent in the very nature of the book of *Jonah*. Our Christian faith and our Christian mission must be seen in their total Judeo-Christian setting. *Jonah* is one of the earliest, clearest and most eloquent expressions of that universal, seeking love that came to earth in a manger and died on a cross to redeem mankind. To call the book anything else than missionary is to deny its true character. It is missionary in the broadest sense of this term, for it speaks to the total church in total mission at home and abroad. It is both centripetal and centrifugal. It shows that the mission field is not exclusively "out yonder" somewhere, but is "right

17

here" as well. The mission field is wherever people are in rebellion against God.

Jonah speaks to our day in a way that is nothing less than startling. The human problems that the book faces are peculiarly our problems: the problems of extreme nationalism; the problems of the denial of loving community and the quest for humanization; the problems of cultural and racial relationships; the problems of rebellion against God and the resulting storms that have swept across our twentieth century; the problems of our small concepts of God, our narrow provincialisms, our consuming unconcern, and our aloofness from involvement in the hurt of humanity. For the Christian, likewise, the book raises the question of our motive for mission. As in the days of old, God speaks through his prophet—if we will listen. What specifically does the book of *Jonah* have to say to our generation? There seem to be seven basic themes:[22]

1. God's sovereignty and love are universal. He rules the Ninevites as well as the Israelites; his demand for righteousness applies to all. Likewise, his love and his mercy are for all people regardless of racial or national origin.

2. We cannot escape God. We may defy God, as did the Ninevites, or flee from God, as did Jonah, but we cannot escape. Both the Ninevites in their wickedness and Jonah in his flight are the subjects of God's sovereign power and his loving mercy.

3. All people are equal before God. The Jew has no favored position. When Gentiles repent, they are saved and occupy the same place as the Jew in God's kingdom.

4. God's action is primary. All are completely dependent upon God for salvation.

5. The door to salvation is repentance.

6. In the exercise of his sovereign grace, God has chosen Israel to carry his message of judgment and mercy to all the nations. This is Israel's mission in the world.

7. God's forgiving grace and love are without limits, extending to all in spite of Israel's refusal to fulfill its misson. God's love and his redeeming work are not limited by the narrowness of his chosen people.

We now turn to a detailed development of this message as it is expressed in the story of Jonah.

Study Questions

1. Explain the Old Testament use of the phrase "Word of the Lord."

2. What is the primary meaning of the word *prophecy* in the Old Testament?

3. How has the fish incident distorted the message of *Jonah*? Is this incident central in the story of *Jonah*? Why? Why not?

4. Who was Jonah and when did he live?

5. Who wrote the book of *Jonah* and when was it written?

6. Describe the conditions that made Assyria, of which Nineveh was capital, a bitter enemy of Israel.

7. The author says, "The high-water mark of Hebrew prophecy was reached just before, during and after the exile." Describe the way in which this came about, stating the two causes of the rise of ethical monotheism in this period.

8. Describe the two divergent opinions that grew up in post-exilic Israel around the way the people should reestablish and keep the covenant with Yahweh. Show how this controversy provided the occasion for the writing of *Jonah*. What two antithetical movements arose out of this controversy?

9. Discuss the literary character of *Jonah,* showing how it is history, parable and allegory.

10. Discuss the book of *Jonah* as a missionary treatise.

11. State the seven points that comprise the basic message of *Jonah*.

12. A good question around which to organize the rest of the study would be: What is my mission and the mission of my church today?

Exegesis

1:1 *Word:* The word of God in the Old Testament is identified with God's action and his being. *Genesis,* Chapter I, reads: "God said . . . and there was . . ." His word is his power. A word once spoken by God accomplishes its purpose (*Isaiah 55*:11). It is therefore a serious thing to place oneself in opposition to the declared word of God. The poignancy and excitement of the book of *Jonah* is that Jonah, the most arrogant, self-willed and unyielding character of the entire Bible, sets his head to defy the word of God.

Came to: The Hebrew expression here can be translated "is." "The word of the LORD *is* to Jonah."

LORD: The word *LORD,* spelled with all capital letters is used in the Revised Standard Version and the King James Version to translate the Hebrew name *Yahweh*[23] (sometimes written "Jehovah"). For a discussion of the name Yahweh and how the terms *LORD* and *Jehovah* came to be used, see footnote.

Word of the LORD: A phrase commonly used in the Old Testament to introduce prophecy. Compare *Jeremiah* 1:2, 4; *Hosea* 1:1, *Joel* 1:1; *Micah* 1:1; *Zephaniah* 1:1; *Haggai* 1:1; *Zechariah* 1:1; *Malachi* 1:1. *Amos* 1:3 says "Thus says the LORD"; and *Isaiah* 1:2, "The LORD has spoken." In using the phrase, the author stresses the fact that *Jonah* stands in the same tradition as the other great prophetic books of Israel. The book does not center in the miracle of Jonah's deliverance from the fish (as many have supposed), but on the fact that God is speaking through the prophet. "Prophecy" in our day has come to mean in popular usage "foretelling the future," but in the Old Testament times it meant primarily "speaking forth the word of God." In contrast to most of the prophetic books there is no superscription or title to the book of *Jonah.* Verse 1:1 is an integral part of the narrative.

Footnotes

[1] Copyrighted by Joseph Bindar, 1956.

[2] George Adam Smith, *The Book of the Twelve Prophets* (New York: George H. Doran Co., n.d.), II, p. 492.

[3] C. H. Cornill, *The Prophets of Israel* (Chicago: 1897), p. 170.

[4] Costen J. Harrell, *The Prophets of Israel* (Nashville: Cokesbury Press, 1933), p. 227.

[5] Smith, *op. cit.,* p. 495.

[6] Quoted by Charles A. Dinsmore, *The English Bible at Literature* (Boston: Houghton Mifflin Co., 1931), p. 256.

[7] George L. Robinson, *The Twelve Prophets* (New York: Geo. H. Doran Co., 1926), p. 89.

[8] This is the view generally held among scholars. An important attempt to date Jonah in the pre-exilic period has been made recently by George M. Landes, Union Theological Seminary, New York City, in an unpublished manuscript.

[9] This is an oversimplified summary of Israelite history. See Norman K. Gottwald, *A Light to the Nations* (New York: Harper and Brothers, 1959), pp. 180-214.

[10] Jaques Ellul, *The Judgment of Jonah* (Grand Rapids, Michigan: William B. Eerdmans, 1971), p. 26.

[11] As noted previously, some scholars (i.e., George M. Landes, Union

Theological Seminary, New York) are now arguing for a pre-exilic dating for the composition of Jonah. For the purposes of this study, the dating makes little difference since the attitudes toward non-Jews were essentially the same in both periods. In fact, the hatred of the Assyrians was probably greater before the exile than after.

[12] The word *universalism* is used in the ordinary sense and has no connection here with the theological doctrine of universal salvation.

[13] The book of *Isaiah* contains the writings of at least two persons. Chapters 1-39 are attributed to First Isaiah. Chapters 40-66 were written at a later time. Some attribute 40-55 to Second Isaiah (sometimes referred to as Deutero-Isaiah) and 56-66 to still another writer or writers. For a further discussion, see Gottwald, *op. cit.,* pp. 400-402.

[14] There are some scholars who now contend that *Ruth* and *Job* are pre-exilic writings. For *Job* see: Marvin H. Pope, *Job,* a volume in The Anchor Bible series (New York: Doubleday, 1965), pp. xxx-xxxvii. For *Ruth* see: Edward S. Campbell, Jr., Vol VII in The Anchor Bible Series (New York: Doubleday, 1975).

[15] This same concept of Yahweh is expressed in almost the same words in the following passages: *Numbers* 14:18, *Deuteronomy* 4:31, *Nehemiah* 9:17, *Psalms* 86:15, 103:8, 145:8.

[16] Robert Funk, discussing the situational aspect of the parable when considered as metaphor, points out that it is not quite correct to say that the parable has only one ideational point, because a parable interprets the situation rather than the parable itself being "interpreted" in an ideational way. It is only possible to say that the parable has "one point" in the sense of its having a basic thrust or impact to which all aspects of the parable point. Funk says, "It is thus possible—I say 'possible' to indicate that prudence is required—to affirm that the parable, as metaphor, has not one but many 'points,' as many points as there are situations into which it is spoken. . . . The emphasis on one point over against the allegorization of the parables was a necessary corrective, but one point understood as an idea valid for all times is . . . erroneous" (*Language, Hermeneutic and Word of God.* New York: Harper and Row, 1966, p. 151).

[17] *The New Century Bible,* ed. R. F. Horton (Edinburgh: T. C. and E. C. Jack, n.d.), Vol. I, p. 199.

[18] For a more complete discussion of the question of the historicity of Jonah, see Appendix II, p. 128.

[19] *A Commentary on the Bible,* ed., Arthur S. Peake (London: Thomas Nelson and Sons, 1919), p. 556.

[20] Johannes Blauw, *The Missionary Nature of the Church* (New York: McGraw-Hill Book Co., Inc., 1962), pp. 33 ff.

[21] Hans-Ruedi Weber, *The Invitation, Matthew on Mission* (New York: Joint Commission on Education and Cultivation, Board of Missions of The United Methodist Church, 1971).

[22] We are not unmindful of other themes in *Jonah.* For example, it has been suggested that the book serves the apologetic purpose of showing why the prophecies against heathen nations were not always fulfilled. Another suggestion is that the book is an attempt to set forth the true nature of the prophetic calling along three lines: (1) the prophet must perform whatever God commands him, however unusual it appears; (2) even death cannot nullify his calling; (3) the prophet has no right to the fulfillment of prediction, but must place it in God's hand. (See Frederick Carl Eiselen, *The Minor Prophets,* New York: Eaton and Mains, 1907, pp. 327-332). Others have suggested that the book is a satire on the Hebrew prophet. These themes and others may have their place in the story, but they are subordinate to the main themes as outlined here.

[23] For readers not familiar with the term *Yahweh* a word of explanation may be helpful. It is considered by scholars to be probably the correct pronunciation of the Hebrew word for God sometimes pronounced "Jehovah." In ancient Hebrew only the consonants were written, and the reader supplied the vowel sounds. So the name for God appeared as YHWH, called the "Tetragrammaton" meaning four letters. Early in the Christian era a group of Hebrew scribes known as the Masoretes added vowel signs to the consonants of the Old Testament Hebrew text indicating the traditional pronunciation. However, they did not add signs to the YHWH, since the name had come to be considered too sacred to be pronounced. Instead they attached vowel signs indicating that where the YHWH appeared one should say "Adonai" (the first "a" has the sound of "e" as in equity), which means "Lord." In time the vowels of the Hebrew word *Adonai* came to be incorporated into the YHWH, with the result that in the late medieval period the form *Jehovah* appeared. The "Y" sound is represented by "J" and the "W" sound by "V", as in Latin. Thus the word *Jehovah* is a hybrid which combines the consonants of the YHWH with the vowels of the Hebrew *Adonai*. The only English version that makes wide use of *Jehovah* is the American Revised Version published in 1901. The older King James Version uses the phrase "THE LORD" (except in seven places). In this book we will use the original YHWH with the pronunciation Yahweh.

II
REBEL

"Jonah, the Son of Amittai": God's Call

Now the word of the LORD came to Jonah the son of Amittai, saying, "Arise, go to Nineveh, that great city, and cry against it; for their wickedness has come up before me."

—Jonah 1:1-2.

George Bernard Shaw used to say that the Bible is more up to date than the morning's newspaper. Its characters are both timeless and universal. Sarah Henderson Hay writes:

> Stone crumbles but more staunchly fares
> A dust incredibly translated:
> Judas still haggles at his wares,
> Cain is forever new created.
> Delilah, in a Paris frock
> Goes out to tea at five o'clock;
> Salome climbs the subway stairs;
> Potiphar takes the elevated.[1]

One of the characters you will meet most is Jonah. He walks every street, boards every bus and every ship and flees to every modern Tarshish. The Bible calls him "Jonah, the son of Amittai." Names in ancient Israel almost always carried symbolical meanings. Abraham means "exalted father"; Joshua (Jesus) means "salvation"; Bethel means "house of God"; Immanuel, "God with us"; Jonah is the Hebrew word for dove. *Amittai* is a secondary form of the Hebrew word *emeth,* which means truth or faithfulness. *Son of* is used in the Bible in the ordinary way, but it also sometimes carries the connotation of "one who exemplifies the qualities of" or "one who is filled with the spirit of" (note *Psalms* 89:22, *Isaiah* 14:12, *Luke* 10:6,

23

Acts 4:36, *II Thessalonians* 2:3). *Jonah the son of Amittai,* therefore, in Hebrew symbolism can mean "dove filled with the spirit of truth and faithfulness." Also in Hebrew symbolism a dove is a messenger, as in the story of Noah's ark, and Israel is sometimes thought of as a dove. The symbolism of the dove at the baptism of Jesus is significant in this connection. The dove as a messenger symbolizes the coming of the Holy Spirit upon Jesus as he sets out on his earthly mission. Jonah's name, therefore, symbolizing Israel, suggests that Israel is a "messenger of truth and faithfulness."

We should note in passing that some Old Testament scholars question the identification of Israel with the dove.[2] However, when the entire message of Jonah is taken into consideration, it seems apparent that the author of the book uses the prophet Jonah and his name with such symbolism in mind. Jonah's name stands for faithfulness to the God of truth, but like Israel, he is unfaithful. He runs from his responsibility. The entire focus of the book is on the irony of a man named "truth and faithfulness" running from God and defying God. Therefore, if we are to grasp the meaning of the book of *Jonah,* we must see it as it applies to the life of Israel. Scholars differ as to the details of this application, but most agree that *Jonah's* message is to be found in the setting of Israel's relationship to the nation around it. Some scholars, for example, see in *Jonah* direct symbolical references to the Babylonian captivity and the exile. Others view such supposed symbolism as inaccurate. Some see the raging sea and the big fish that swallowed Jonah as representative of the Babylonian power which "swallowed" Judah (note *Jeremiah* 51:34 ff). Others reject this interpretation. Whereas the symbolism of the sea seems appropriate in that the sea, like Babylon, swallowed up to destroy, the symbolism of the fish does not seem appropriate in that the big fish swallowed Jonah to save his life, not to destroy it. Thus, those who reject the allegorical interpretation of *Jonah* insist that though there are parallels in terminology between *Jonah* and *Jeremiah* 51:34, 42, 44-45 (a description of the exile that we will look at shortly), there are also differences, and it is not proper to connect *Jonah* and *Jeremiah* in any direct way.

On the other hand, there are scholars, who, while not pressing for a literal correspondence, nevertheless see what they feel are valid literary parallels. They believe that a broad range of the experiences of Israel are symbolized in the story of *Jonah*. They point out that a number of passages in the Old Testament depict the sea and its monsters as opposing Yahweh, such as *Psalms* 46:3, 74:13, 89:9; *Isaiah* 27:1, 51:9-10; and *Job* 7:12, 26:12-13. The same symbolism is observed in the book of *Revelation* where John, speaking of the day of final victory, says, "And the sea was no more" (*Revelation* 21:1). Therefore, they think that the writer of *Jonah* saw the storm and the raging sea which were caused by Yahweh as a judgment on Jonah, as in some sense representing the hostile powers that Israel's prophets saw as Yahweh's instruments of judgment on Israel. If we look at Jeremiah's description of the Babylonian captivity, certain parallels, at least on the surface, seem apparent:

> Nebuchadrezzar the king of Babylon has devoured me,
>   he has crushed me;
> he has made me an empty vessel,
>   he has swallowed me like a monster;
> he has filled his belly with my delicacies,
>   he has rinsed me out. . . .
> And I will punish Bel in Babylon,
>   and take out of his mouth what he has swallowed.
> The nations shall no longer flow to him;
>   the wall of Babylon has fallen.
> "Go out of the midst of her, my people!
>
>   (*Jeremiah* 51:34, 44-45a)

It is, of course, possible that all seeming parallels between this passage and *Jonah* are purely coincidental. It should be noted that whereas *Jonah* uses the Hebrew word "dag" (fish), which does not carry hostile connotations, *Jeremiah* uses the Hebrew word "tannin" (sea serpent or sea monster) which does carry hostile connotations. However, that there are striking parallels cannot be denied. It is, of course, quite possible that the passage in *Jeremiah* is a reflection of the theme in *Jonah* rather than vice versa, in which case *Jonah* must be dated before the exile. Or both passages may reflect an independent tradition. The present writer believes that it is not necessary to press for any literal connection between *Jonah* and *Jeremiah* in order to see the thematic similarity and to affirm that the author of *Jonah* used his story to symbolize the experiences of Israel, not only in regard to the exile, but also in regard to many other aspects of Israel's life. Obviously we cannot press any of the symbolism for literal correspondence, and certainly not that of the fish. Nevertheless, while the fish clearly is the means of Jonah's salvation, the experience in the belly of the fish was itself, in this writer's opinion, most unpleasant—not too unlike the exile. We will observe in subsequent chapters how Jonah's entire experience is used by the author to depict Israel's relationships to the Gentile world. The people of Israel escaped from the exile. However, even after their miraculous deliverance, many were still unwilling to carry out God's mission. They sought to cut themselves off from the hated heathen. They desired the destruction of the heathen, not their salvation. Like Jonah after his deliverance from the raging sea, they sat and pouted when God showed his mercy and revealed his love. They drew more rigid the lines of separation and built higher the barricades that thwarted God's loving purpose for all mankind. They shut God's love in and shut God's people out.

Jonah, son of Amittai (that is, Israel), was the messenger of God's truth to all the world. Yet Israel, chosen for a purpose, now demanded a privilege—the privilege of separation from the world into the smug complacency of its own favored position. God was determined to shock the Israelites out of this complacency and to send them into the world. He raised up a prophet, Jonah, the son of Amittai, and sent him out to Nineveh. The church today, likewise sent into the world, has often fled to Tarshish—to the security of its sanctuaries, the subtleties of its theology and the vested interests of its institutional life. The message of *Jonah* is needed today to shock the church out of this complacency and to thrust it into the world.

God is ever struggling to make clear that his people—his covenant community—are "messengers of truth." This is at the heart of the entire biblical revelation. We today, no less than ancient Israel, are "Jonah, the son of Amittai." We are sent upon a mission to the world. It is God's mission. We are a part of what God is doing in his world—or we should be! The question is: are we any more faithful to the task than was ancient Israel? The pages that follow will seek to answer this question. It could be that we will find the message of *Jonah* as shockingly relevant today as it was in 350 B.C.

Study Questions

1. Define and discuss the phrase, "Jonah, Son of Amittai." How does it symbolize the life of Israel?

2. In what ways would you apply the phrase "Jonah, son of Amittai" to the Christian church today?

3. At this stage in your study, how would you define a "Jonah"? Have you met any Jonahs?

4. From your reading thus far, in what ways do you see the message of Jonah "shockingly relevant" to our day? Possibly you can anticipate some of the issues the author will discuss in the following pages.

"Jonah Rose to Flee": Rebellion

But Jonah rose to flee to Tarshish from the presence of the LORD. He went down to Joppa and found a ship going to Tarshish; so he paid the fare, and went on board, to go with them to Tarshish, away from the presence of the LORD.

—Jonah 1:3.

Instead of answering God's call to go to Nineveh Jonah arose and fled in the opposite direction. Nineveh was far to the east. Tarshish was far to the west. As noted in the exegesis, Jonah thought that Yahweh's jurisdiction ended at the boundaries of Israel, or at least that Yahweh's word or commission could not reach him outside Israel. The phrase, "from the presence of the LORD," is used twice in verse 3. The author wants to make clear that Jonah is trying to escape God and thus to escape the demands of God upon him as an acknowledged prophet. To remain in God's presence, the author is saying, would demand that Jonah surrender his deepseated prejudices and give up his morbid, burning desire for vengeance on his hated enemies, the Ninevites. This Jonah could never think of doing. Impulsively he leaped to his feet and ran in order to escape this impossible demand. The author is contending that Israel's narrow, vengeful attitude is actually an act of running from God, a rejection of God.

Jonah's aim was to go as far as he could. Tarshish was the

"jumping off place." It was the end of the world. There was nothing halfway about his rebellion. In this Jonah was like us today for we have rebelled in many extreme ways. Some of us have even dared attempt to usurp God's throne and declare God dead. Jonah's rebellion was like ours in another way, too, for it was a rebellion that masqueraded as obedience. Through all of his defiance, he continued to present himself as a true prophet of God. He insisted that he "feared the LORD." Verse 2:1 says, "Then Jonah prayed." Thus, the most conspicuous forms of piety covered his total rejection of God's will. We, in the twentieth century, may have dispensed with many of the pious forms of prayer, but we still masquerade our rebellion as obedience. We can always find pious purposes for pursuing personal goals. It matters not whether the forms of piety are old-fashioned sacred forms or new-fashioned secular, worldly forms; they may still cover up the most brazen assertion of self and the most complete rejection of God's will.

Some writers have seen Jonah's going to Nineveh as a chastened submission to the will of God, making him a model for us to follow, or have even seen him as a "type of Christ" to emulate. The present writer fails to find any evidence for this kind of interpretation. Note that though Jonah did go to Nineveh after his experience with the fish, not once did he ever actually submit to God's will. He rebelled to the very end. The view that Jonah's going to Nineveh was submission to God overlooks the fact, as we will see below, that Jonah went not in submission, but because he hoped (*Jonah* 4) to force God to submit to his (Jonah's) will and destroy the Ninevites.

Rather than exemplifying obedience at this point, Jonah seems to show the tragic rebellion of a man who down to the very end would rather die than submit to God's will. The traditional view held among both conservative and liberal scholars that Jonah "repented" and "obeyed" God is therefore a serious misreading of the book. Likewise, the sentimental sermonizing that has made Jonah a type of Christ must be re-thought. There was not a single way in which Jonah was like Jesus. Jesus wept over the death of one man, Lazarus. Jonah pouted because God refused to kill a half-million people. Jesus called men to repentance. Jonah became exceedingly angry when a half-million sinners did repent. Jesus said, "Let the little children come unto me." Jonah said, "Destroy them. Rain down fire and brimstone." Jesus died to save sinners. Jonah wanted to die rather than see them saved.

What a striking picture of the proud, self-righteous, unrepentant rebel! Jonah, the messenger of truth, was determined to save the world in his own way. He knew perfectly well how to do it: Destroy the Ninevites! They were devils, and the only way you can establish God's kingdom is to do away with devils. How modern this sounds in a world seeking peace, but obsessed with instruments of destruction. Is our twentieth century a Jonah century? Are we so deeply and fundamentally in rebellion against God that we must put on a masquerade of obedience? Are we out to save the world—but in our own way? Like Jonah, are we not sure we know how to do it?

There are volunteers on every hand. We are willing—even anxious—to go forth on a great mission. With high sounding slogans and carloads of schemes, we set out to save the world. We are willing to go to every Tarshish through massive deterrents, defense pacts and foreign aid, wars to "save" people and arms to help them "save" themselves, peace corps, great institutions and elaborate church organizations, demonstrations, marches, fighting communism—anything. We are noted for our activism. Everybody wants to get into the act. We are determined to save the world. We are willing to do anything —except the one thing that is necessary and that is to repent, surrender to God's will and follow God's way. We are wedded to our own wills and divorced from God's will.

This analysis of our current dilemma is contrary to the strong notes in present day theology that seek to celebrate our goodness and self-sufficiency. Certainly we do not wish to belittle in any way either our responsibility for our tragic plight or the right kind of activism designed to do something about conditions that are no longer acceptable in our world. Christians must be deeply involved on the front lines in the struggle for all kinds of human rights such as economic justice and racial equality. But the issues are always complex and often ambiguous. The many manifestations of sin at even the highest levels of the struggle for human rights should teach us humility; the pride and self-righteousness so apparent in many of the demonstrations and the revolt movements of today should place us on our guard; the danger of denying basic human rights under the guise of fighting for human rights cannot be taken lightly; the temptation to use unchristian means to attain supposedly Christian ends; and the widespread eruption of selfishness and greed in the name of fighting for economic justice should remind us at all times that we, too, are sinners. We can easily forget that. One of our most subtle dangers is that we will become Jonahs. Thinking we are the solution we will forget that we are in fact the problem. We will not fail to go, but we will go in the wrong direction. "But Jonah rose to flee."

Study Questions

1. What are some of the ways you are running from God? Be specific. For example, is your complacency that often fails to take seriously such issues as world poverty, economic injustice, racism and women's liberation a running from God?

2. What does the author mean by a rebellion that masquerades as obedience? In what ways may our piety be a cover up for a basic rejection of God's will? For example, can our active church attendance in America be a cover up for our failure to achieve genuine racial harmony? Is a segregated church inherently a rebellion masquerading as obedience? If so, why? If not, why?

3. Why is it that we would rather do something than repent? The author speaks of the "right kind of activism." What would that be? Would it be an activism which recognizes that it is part of the problem as well as part of the solution?

4. Much current theology (spoken of as the "new humanism") stresses our self-sufficiency. It believes we have depended too much on God to solve our problems. Can dependence on God be a block to progress? If so, how? If not, why?

5. Have you observed specific instances of denying human rights under the guise of fighting for human rights? Can this be avoided? In cases of conflict of rights, how are we to judge whose rights to fight for or to preserve?

6. Remembering the discussion in Chapter I, discuss why Jonah refused to accept God's demand that he go to Nineveh.

7. How does God speak to people today to make his demands known? How can we know what is the will of God in specific areas of conflict?

8. Who do we regard as the Ninevites of our day? Why?

"The Lord Hurled a Great Wind":
The Impossibility of Escape

But the LORD hurled a great wind upon the sea, and there was a mighty tempest on the sea, so that the ship threatened to break up.

—Jonah 1:4.

In Chapter I we stated one of the major themes of *Jonah* as follows: "We cannot escape God. We may defy God, as did the Ninevites, or flee from God, as did Jonah, but we cannot escape. Both the Ninevites in their wickedness and Jonah in his flight are the subjects of God's sovereign power and his loving mercy."

Jonah discovered this the hard way. So have we. If contemporary events are teaching us anything, they are teaching us that escape from God is impossible. There are moral laws in the universe just as there are physical laws. We can violate these laws, but we cannot then escape the consequences of our violation. For example, we can violate the laws of love and justice. But having violated these laws we must then accept the inevitable consequences: a world torn by strife, violence, revolution and war. In the words of Hosea, when we sow the wind we can expect to reap the whirlwind (*Hosea* 8:7). The storms that are sweeping across our world today are evidence that we cannot do wrong and get by. We cannot escape God.

Rebellion against God of course is as old as the Garden of Eden, for all sin is at bottom an attempt to usurp the place of God and to be God. The crowning temptation in the Garden of Eden was when the serpent assured Adam, "You shall be like God." Adam and Eve were not content to be creatures in the image of God. They wanted to be God, to be their own God, to set their own standards, to be their own final court of appeal. But their attempt to take the reins of the universe into their own hands has brought nothing but frustration and chaos.

For instance, Louis W. Hodges points out that the hell of racial tensions that continually frustrates all of us roots fundamentally in a "threat orientation," which "is to be understood theologically as the failure of the creature to acknowledge his creaturehood and the concomitant effort to make himself the center of the universe . . . Racial prejudice, therefore, is none other than a manifestation of man's effort to usurp the throne of God. The prejudiced personality sees himself, as well as his race, his collective self-image, as having and meriting powers over his fellow creatures which rightly belong only to the Creator." [3]

This means that to cease rebelling against God is not a matter of saying "yes," of going somewhere or doing something. For as noted above, our basic rebellion is actually a rebellion that masquerades as obedience, as doing and going. To cease our rebellion, rather, is to recognize our creaturehood. It is to recognize that we cannot escape God. It is to submit to God, to surrender to his will, to surrender the inner citadel of our self-hood. But we instinctively—as individuals and as nations—recoil from such self-surrender. For such surrender seems to mean the complete annihilation of self. We cling desperately to the self, to the ego, and to all that supports it, even though this clinging means a distorted view of ourselves and a prejudiced view of others.

We are on the wrong road. We have caught the wrong ship. What we cannot see is that the surrender of the will to God results not in annihilation but in fulfillment. It is the only way authentic selfhood can be found. The *New English Bible* translates Matthew 16:25, "whoever . . . will let himself be lost for my sake, he will find his true self." Though the Greek verb here is active and not passive, the *New English Bible* has caught an essential meaning. Too many of us are going about trying to lose ourselves. Ours is a rebellion that masquerades as obedience. We must surrender—let ourselves be lost in Christ, for this is the key to obedience. It is the exact opposite of what Jonah was trying to do. Jonah was trying to "get lost." He was trying to escape. Even his seeming obedience later in the story was only a masquerade. But escape was impossible. In trying to escape God, Jonah was trying to escape from himself, from his own conscience, but God was persistent. He was patient, longsuffering, but doggedly determined. He never let go and he never gave up.

Jonah is us. The more we run, the more we run into the face of the storm. "For the sea grew more and more tempestuous" (*Jonah* 1:11b). When will we learn that we cannot escape God?

Study Questions

1. Do you agree with Louis Hodges' analysis of the origin of racial prejudice? Why?

2. Can you give out of your observation or personal experience examples of frustrated attempts to run from God?

3. List ways in which you feel we in the twentieth century have sown the wind and are now reaping the whirlwind?

4. Is it ever possible to escape God?

5. Both Nineveh and Jonah were in rebellion against God, though in different ways. Whose rebellion would be the hardest to overcome?

Exegesis

1:1. *Jonah, the son of Amittai:* For a discussion of Jonah's name, see pages 23-24.

1:2. *Nineveh:* Located on the eastern bank of the Tigris River approximately 230 miles north of the present city of Baghdad and just opposite the present city of Mosul. It was ancient in origin, and around 1100 B.C. seems to have become a royal residence. It reached the height of its power in the eighth and seventh centuries B.C. during the lifetime of the prophet Jonah (*II Kings* 14:25) and came to its full grandeur when it was made the capital of Assyria by Sennacherib (705-681 B.C.) It was famed for its palatial buildings, its gold, and its massive walls so thick that two chariots could ride abreast on top of them. Herodotus says the walls were 380 feet high and 80 feet thick. While the height is probably an exaggeration, at one point the thickness likely reached as much as 110 feet. (For further details of the city's size, see Appendix I.) The Assyrian hordes based in Nineveh had pillaged, burned, killed and enslaved the peoples of Palestine on several occasions. Jonah could not have been sent to a more impossible place as far as the Israelites were concerned.

Cry against it: The specific message Jonah is to deliver is not stated. But the words used indicate that it is to be a message of judgment—a clear recognition of Yahweh's sovereignty over all people. (Compare *Isaiah* 6:3, *Jeremiah* 1:10, and *Amos* 1:3, 6, 9, 13.) As noted in chapter one, this principle of Yahweh's sovereignty is crucial for the development of the story.

Come up before me: God, seated on his throne above the earth (the three-story universe), is offended by the stench of Nineveh's wickedness. What the wickedness was is not specified, but an indication may be found in reading Nahum's scathing denunciation of the city, particularly *Nahum* 3:1-7. One may compare *Genesis* 18:21 where God "goes down" to check on the wickedness of Sodom and Gomorrah.

1:3. *Rose to flee:* The specific reason for Jonah's flight is not stated in chapter 1, but it is made clear in 4:2. Jonah suspected from the beginning that God's purpose was to bring about the repentance of the Ninevites and thus their salvation. This was the last thing that Jonah desired.

From the presence of the LORD: The phrase is equivalent to "away from Yahweh's land" or away from the place where Yahweh's presence is felt and his voice heard. It reflects the ancient concept that a god's presence is limited to the geographical area over which he has jurisdiction. *Genesis* 4:16 says, "Then Cain went away from the presence of the LORD, and dwelt in the land of Nod, east of Eden." Compare *I Samuel* 26:19-20; *II Kings* 5:17 and 17:20, 23. In time, the term came to be used figuratively denoting one's spiritual estrangement from God. This transition may be observed in such passages as *Jeremiah* 23:39. For Jonah the escape is not so much from Yahweh's power, which he knows deep down he cannot escape, but from Yahweh's Word and hence from the commission to go to Nineveh.

Joppa: The modern Jaffa, which is the chief port of southern Palestine. It features in early Israelite history (*Joshua* 19:46) and has retained both its name and its present location across the centuries. It was not an Israelite town until captured by Jonathan in 148 B.C. (*I Maccabees* 10:74-76). However, it was used as a port for Jerusalem as early as the time of Solomon. *II Chronicles* 2:16 and *Ezra* 3:7 mention it as the port where the cedars of Lebanon were unloaded for Solomon's temple (see *I Kings* 5:9). It was the home of Dorcas (*Acts* 9:36) and featured prominently in the early church. Likewise it is the place where in Greek mythology Andromeda was chained. Here Peter had his vision that led to the first Gentile convert, Cornelius (*Acts* 10:9-16). Mythologists naturally associate the monster that Perseus slew with Jonah's great fish.

Tarshish: There are several references to Tarshish in the Old Testament. See *Psalms* 48:7 and 72:10; *Isaiah* 2:16 and 23:1; *Ezekiel* 27:12, 25 and 38:13. The word *Tarshish* is Phoenician and means "refinery." Hence a city named Tarshish would have been a refinery port on the Mediterranean. There seem to have been a number of such ports, and it is not certain which is the one referred to in *Jonah.* However, it was at the eastern end of the Mediterranean and may have been located on Sardinia or it may have been the ancient Phoenician settlement in Spain called Tartessos. See *II Chronicles* 9:21; *Isaiah* 23:1, 6, 10; *Jeremiah* 10:9; and *Ezekiel* 27:12 for references to trade with Tarshish.

Paid the fare: The Hebrew uses the feminine pronoun, *her fare,* and some have suggested that Jonah paid the fare of the entire ship, indicating that he was quite wealthy. However, this seems unlikely and is not at all required by the sentence structure. "Her fare" probably means only "the fare required by the ship for a one-way passage to Tarshish."

1:4. *A great wind:* Yahweh sent a storm to block Jonah's flight. Here we see the sharp contrast between Jonah's and the author's views of Yahweh. Jonah's god was a tribal god, limited in his jurisdiction to Israel. The author of *Jonah,* in contrast, sees Yahweh as the ruler of the entire world. He can "hurl a storm" wherever and whenever he wishes. The idea that God sends calamity as a punishment is common in the Old Testament. For example, see *Amos* 4:6-11.

Threatened: The Hebrew construction personifies the ship. Literal translation would be: "Thought itself to be broken in pieces."

Footnotes

[1] Sarah Henderson Hay, "Sic Transit," from *Field of Honor* (Kaleidograph Press, 1933). Efforts to locate the copyright holder have been unsuccessful to date.

[2] T. Henshaw, *The Latter Prophets* (London: George Allen and Unwin Ltd., 1958), pp. 288-89.

[3] Article in *Christian Advocate,* March 1, 1962.

III
CRISIS

"Jonah . . . Was Fast Asleep": Lethargy

*Then the mariners were afraid, and each cried to his god;
and they threw the wares that were in the ship into the sea,
to lighten it for them. But Jonah had gone down into the inner
part of the ship and had lain down, and was fast asleep.*
—Jonah 1:5.

When the storm came, Jonah was fast asleep. With the
blankets pulled over his head he slept on. The tempest raged.
The sailors threw the cargo overboard. They prayed to every
god they knew. Jonah, unaware, slept on. The waves lashed.
The ship lurched. Sails ripped. Mast poles crashed. Hell broke
loose. Jonah slept. A Greek translation of the Old Testament
made around 200 B.C. (called the Septuagint) says he was
snoring. He was sleeping through a storm which his own sin
had brought about.

Rip Van Winkle is one of our most contemporary literary
figures. Jonah slept through a storm, Rip through a revolution.
Their modern counterparts are doing both. Halford Luccock has
reminded us that when Rip Van Winkle went up the mountain
there was a picture of George III of England on the wall of the
village inn. When he returned (after twenty years of quiet
sleep), the picture was of another George—George Washington. Rip slept through a revolution. Everything was changed,
but he did not know it. It was a new world, but he was still
living in the old.[1] Today is a new world, but we insist on living
in the old.

Across the world a rebel cry is being heard which actually
was born two hundred years ago among another people under
colonial rule: "We hold these truths to be self-evident, that

all men are created equal, that they are endowed by their creator with certain inalienable rights. . . ." Today's down-trodden peoples in all countries, including the U.S.A., have dared actually to believe this—only to find that many among the descendants of those who coined the slogan now repudiate it.

U Nu, former Premier of Burma, speaking a few years ago at Independence Hall in Philadelphia, reminded us that:

> "In all parts of the world where men live under tyranny, or under foreign domination or in feudal bondage, those who dream and plot and fight for freedom do so in the name of the eternal principles for which your Revolution was fought. . . . the ideas of the American Revolution are . . . more explosive in their capacity to change the world than B-52's or even atomic bombs." [2]

But the U.S.A., born in revolution and dedicated to liberty, has moved so far from her revolutionary origins that in many cases today she has become the U.S.Q.—the United Status Quo. The cry among a billion former colonial subjects, mostly brown and black peoples of Asia, Africa and the Americas, is for the recognition of human dignity and equality. For the most part they have been granted political independence, but the white man has been much slower to respect human dignity. Various forms of segregation and discrimination against peoples of color continue to exist in all parts of the world. Independence is important to any person, but respect for human dignity is far more important.

The day for a bold and daring move into a new world of genuine equality and of complete social and economic justice has come. True, there are dangers involved in new and untried paths. But there are far greater dangers in sitting on the status quo—as we have found out in China, in the Congo, in Cuba, in New York, in Selma, Alabama, in Watts (Los Angeles), in Detroit, in Vietnam, in the universities, in the slums, in the ghettos, in Wounded Knee and everywhere across the world. One fact stands out: the status quo is doomed. Worldwide revolution is upon us—the U.S.A., Latin America, Africa, Asia, everywhere. "But Jonah . . . was fast asleep."

Our sleep sometimes shows itself in a dramatic way. While I was home on furlough from the Philippines, I went to a lovely church in a lovely university town. The people were wonderfully gracious. The stained glass windows were magnificent, the organ inspiring, the carpets luxurious. But somehow we seemed to be way off on the sidelines, while the rushing, raging currents of life passed us by. In the whole area revolution was brewing. The rumblings were clear and ominous. And not long afterward it came with racial violence and death. But in the church that Sunday morning we seemed so quiet, so secure, so isolated from all of this. We were not only segregated from peoples of color, but also isolated from the realities of life.

As the stately service proceeded, I had the eerie feeling one gets in a mausoleum. The brass donation plates on the highly polished pews seemed to read, "R.I.P."—Rest in Peace. A kind of sleepy haze filled the atmosphere. The pastor's announcement that I would now give the morning message brought me back to reality. But as I rose to speak, I felt like rushing to the pulpit and shouting with thunderous voice the words of the ship captain to Jonah, "What do you mean, you sleeper[s]? Arise, call upon your god! Perhaps the god will give a thought to us, that we do not perish." (*Jonah* 1:6).

Study Questions

1. In what ways is the church asleep in your home town? How are individual Christians asleep in our world today?

2. Is the church in your community facing squarely the issues of poverty? racial inclusiveness? housing? women's rights? drugs? other issues?

3. In what ways has the slumber of the church allowed injustice to continue?

4. As the church and church people become more affluent, they have a greater stake in maintaining things as they are. Does this lull the church to sleep? If so, how? In this connection read *Revelation* 3:14-18 and *Ephesians* 5:14.

5. Does obedience to God sometimes make it necessary to rebel? Explain.

"Arise, Call Upon Your God": Idolatry

> So the captain came and said to him, "What do you mean, you sleeper? Arise, call upon your god! Perhaps the god will give a thought to us, that we do not perish."
> —Jonah 1:6.

What a picture! Jonah, running from God, is challenged by a heathen ship captain to call upon his god. But what kind of god did Jonah have? That is, how did Jonah conceive of God? The answer is that Jonah thought of God as a tribal god. The ship captain's reference to "the god" (1:6) subtly placed Jonah's god on a level with all the others. And the irony is that Jonah himself, in fleeing from God, was doing precisely that.

It is true that Jonah speaks about believing in the "God of heaven, who made the sea and the dry land" (1:9). Theoretically, Jonah had a great God, for the God of Israel was and is a great God. And actually Jonah knew this God. Verse 4:2 shows that he knew all along the true nature of God. Israel had "amittai," that is, truth. It was this true knowledge of God—his universal love and mercy—which Israel was rebelling against, as is seen in the contradiction between its clear monotheistic faith and the narrow particularism that denied it. Jonah was like so many today: professing a great faith while living by small concepts. Few today would actually profess faith in a tribal god—but many live by such a faith. The author of Jonah, then, speaks to the heart of one of the twentieth century's deepest problems when he lays bare our small concepts of God.

One of the great debates in current theology revolves around the question of God. How do we understand God today? In our attempts to build a "better" world, have we pushed God aside to find gods more in keeping with our own ideas? It happened for Jonah. Jonah knew the real God (verse 4:2), but having pushed this God aside, he worshipped an idol—his tribal god who was only a magnified image of himself and his nation. It is happening today. Aldous Huxley points out in *Science, Liberty and Peace* that one strange result of scientific progress has been the reversion of monotheism to local idolatries.[3] J. B. Phillips in his book *Your God is Too*

Small, says ". . . there is always a danger of imagining a god with moral qualities like our own, vastly magnified and purified of course, and with the same blind spots." [4]

Jonah, in contrast to the high monotheism of the Second Isaiah, represented the narrow tribalism of ancient Israel, and Jonah's god had Jonah's blind spots. Does the same thing happen today? An African student leaving the United States after a period of study was asked what he had learned about religion. His reply was: "I have learned that God is an American, a white man, a Methodist, and a Republican." [5] A clergyman, as reported in *Newsweek,* confirmed this tribal idea of deity when he said, "If there is anything the Bible teaches, it teaches segregation. No one believes in segregation as much as God." [6] Truly God is a "white man"!

Over against our concepts stands the God of the Christian revelation. The Bible uses personal categories in speaking of God that may appear inadequate, as are all human categories, but they are the best we have. Certainly they are bold and daring categories. The biblical revelation is bold to declare a great God. He is the Supreme Being, the Creator. He is the God of infinite might and limitless love. His power and his love are manifest in the paradox of the cross—in weakness and suffering. He is involved with his creation. He is not only the Creator, but also the Redeemer of his creation. His love knows no bounds. His forgiveness has no limits. His compassion encompasses the earth. He has one demand of all: love.

The message of Jonah is that God's love extends even to the Ninevites. It is the message that finds its most complete expression in the familiar words of John's Gospel: "For God so loved the world that he gave his only Son, that whoever believes in him should not perish but have eternal life" (John 3:16).

How big is your God? At what point do you limit his love? At the boundaries of the ground of your own being? At the boundaries of your family? Your religion or denomination? Your nation? Your race? Your social group? What kind of a god would you call upon if a ship captain rushed up to you in a storm and demanded: "Arise, call upon your god!"?

Study Questions

1. How does our concept of God determine what we are?

How does it determine our relationships to our fellow human beings?

2. Is our God too small? If so, in what ways? Do we still have tribal concepts of God today? Explain.

3. If persons everywhere actually recognized that we are all God's children (as we profess to believe), would this make a difference in our attitudes toward peoples of other races and nations? How?

4. Is the Christian concept of God too small? If not, why not?

"Of What People Are You?": Pride

And they said to one another, "Come, let us cast lots, that we may know on whose account this evil has come upon us." So they cast lots, and the lot fell upon Jonah. Then they said to him, "Tell us, on whose account this evil has come upon us? What is your occupation? And whence do you come? What is your country? And of what people are you?"
                                                          —Jonah 1:7-8

In asking the question, "Of what people are you," the sailors were, of course, wanting to know Jonah's nationality. However, I believe it is not too much of an inference to assume that they also detected an air of pride and arrogance in Jonah, for certainly this trait becomes quite clear as the story progresses. Arnold Toynbee states:

One of the besetting infirmities of living creatures is egotism . . . [and] this self-centeredness generates an illusion. Every soul, tribe, and sect believes itself to be a chosen vessel; and the falsity of our belief in our own unique value does not easily become apparent to us. We can see the fallacy readily, though, when it is a case of somebody else hugging this illusion about himself." [7]

For most of us, the world is made up of two kinds of people: we, the superior ones and they, the inferior ones. Such distinction is usually based on one or more of four things: race, nationality, class, or religious creed. Jews were sure they were superior to Gentiles, including Greeks and Romans. Greeks and Romans were equally sure they were superior to barbarians, including Jews. The superiority complex of the Roman Empire rubbed off on the Christian church at Rome and soon the bishop of Rome began claiming supremacy over the Eastern bishops. The Eastern bishops in turn were perfectly sure that the Eastern church with its intellectual finesse and its theological prowess was superior to the more rough-hewn and barbaric peoples of the West.

The British in the eighteenth and nineteenth centuries were quite sure that they were superior to the Chinese, while the Chinese in turn were equally sure that they were superior to the bearded "foreign devils" who invaded their shores. K. M. Panikkar, an Asian historian, writes, "Two wars had to be fought before the Chinese could think of European nations as anything more than barbarian tribes occupying the outer regions of civilization." [8] To the Chinese, China was the "Celestial Empire," the center of the universe, and the Chinese people were superior to all others. Panikkar points out that "Imperial Commissioner Lin, addressing Queen Victoria in 1842, speaks in all seriousness and honesty of her being the 'Chieftainess of the tribe.' " [9]

In like manner, the Japanese thought of themselves as descendants of the sun goddess, Amaterasu, and thus quite superior to all others. The Germans were convinced that they were the master race. Hitler sought to exterminate Jews as inferior swine and to establish German rule over the entire world. We in the United States have been no exception. We have felt ourselves superior, and it has been clearly apparent to others, most of all when we ourselves have been unaware of it.

A few years ago some U.S. journalists wrote a best seller titled *The Ugly American*.[10] It described both the desirable and the undesirable American overseas. One of its main thrusts was to point up the subtle feelings of superiority and aloofness which dominate many of us and which are often but thinly disguised. The ugly American as portrayed in the book was actually the desirable overseas American. Ugly referred to his physical appearance. Unlike most of his tribe, he was not suave, sophisticated and dumb. On the contrary he was down-to-earth, highly intelligent, friendly, and effective. However, by an interesting twist, the expression "ugly American" quickly came to symbolize the undesirable overseas American, the one who is ugly in spirit. It spoke to the mood of "anti-Americanism" (that is, "anti-U.S.A." feeling) that was rapidly rising at the time. The term clearly pointed to a stereotype, but it also pointed to one of our deepest problems, the problem of false pride and of the unconscious feelings of superiority it engenders.

In our pride we have often thought that our little world was the whole world. At the end of the baseball season each year we play a "World Series" in which only U.S. teams are involved. For years our studies in "world history" and "world civilization" mentioned nothing east of Persia or west of San Francisco, except for an occasional reference to Marco Polo, Ghengis Khan, or some colonial event that affected the west. Norman Cousins, editor of *Saturday Review World*, speaking at the University of the Philippines in Manila, said, "I am a half-educated man—educated to live in only half the world." [11]

U.S. citizens are not the only ones who have this problem, but we must frankly face the question: have our attitudes toward other peoples been a block to the kingdom of God? Has the question "Of what people are you?" so dominated our relationships that we have unconsciously, but nevertheless in fact, tried to shut God's people out and shut God's love in? Thousands in Africa and Asia have turned in recent years to Islam, Buddhism or some other religion, saying that they have been shut out of the "white man's religion"—Christianity.

The writer of *Jonah* was saying that the Israelites in their desire to preserve their rich heritage, which was laudable enough, were nevertheless making a fatal mistake. They were building a wall instead of a bridge, cutting people out rather than including them in. The attempt at preservation was becoming perversion. Have we acted similarly in our desire to preserve our rich heritage? Have we built walls and drawn lines and cut people out because of class or color or race or style of life? Have we drawn lines too rigid in our effort to preserve democracy and "contain" communism?

We have divided east from west, north from south, black from white, rich from poor. The writer of *Jonah* was saying, "Tear down the walls, uproot the fences, embrace the world— even the Ninevites!" Tearing down the ugly walls which today separate us from each other and from God is our supreme task, for God does not like walls. "For he is our peace, who has made us both one, and has broken down the dividing wall of hostility" (*Ephesians* 2:14). In Christ we no longer even think of asking the question, "Of what people are you?" We already know. Everyone belongs to Christ. "For all things are yours, . . . and you are Christ's; and Christ is God's" (*I Corinthians* 3:21-23).

Study Questions

1. How can we help to tear down cultural and racial walls that divide people in our own community? in our schools? in our church?

2. How does the question "Of what people are you?" determine a person's place in your community if the answer is: Italian? Chinese? Indian? Negro? Mexican? Catholic? Protestant? Muslim? Jew? Arab? Some other minority group?

3. Is the dream of a world community an illusion? Why or why not? If we are ever to have a world community what is necessary?

4. What can be done about economic and political walls that keep an oppressive police state in power and buttress an unjust economic order? Is violent revolution the only answer? What are the alternatives?

"I Am A Hebrew": Heritage

And he said to them, "I am a Hebrew; and I fear the LORD, the God of heaven, who made the sea and the dry land."   —Jonah 1:9

"I am a Hebrew and I fear the LORD." What shocking hypocrisy! How could Jonah say that he reverenced the LORD when he was in the very act of defying him? In spite of this hypocrisy, however, there is a sense in which Jonah did fear the LORD. He was no doubt strict in his observance of the Law. In all probability he adhered to high moral and ethical principles. Among these principles was an emphasis on the importance of his national and religious heritage. Jonah was proud of this heritage, and he was determined to preserve it.

Jonah had reason to be proud. As we have observed, his was a great heritage. Therefore, in order to be fair, we must see the other side of the picture. Pride has its virtue as well

44

as its vice. The breadth of the book of *Jonah* is nowhere more in evidence than in the fact that it presents both sides. Indeed, the author had such a profound appreciation of the Hebrew heritage that he was unwilling to see it dissipated. This was the whole purpose of his writing. He was boldly proclaiming the true genius of the Hebrew heritage over against those who were perverting it.

The Jewish people felt bound by a deep sense of responsibility to preserve their rich heritage. What they did not realize was that preserving a heritage can never be achieved by isolation or by a static stand on the status quo. It involves growth and change. It demands the courage to discard old forms in the creative task of making great truths eternally relevant to new situations. Such courage is demanded today. At no time in history has there been greater upheaval in society. A theology that is relevant must be revolutionary. Old encrusted forms must be broken, and the new must be ushered in. But the basic question remains: How can we preserve that which is valid and essential while discarding that which is a block to the fulfillment of God's purpose? We confront the same fundamental issue which the Hebrews confronted.

For example, one of the real dangers in America today is that when the storms of fury over desegregation, student power, black power, the eradication of poverty, the achievement of economic justice, have spent their force, the country, purged and purified in many ways, may nevertheless be left denuded of a priceless heritage—the heritage of a deep and meaningful personal character in the culture. The impartial and idealistic forces that proudly overlook the color of a person's face may also forget that he or she has a face. They may accept a person as a citizen and reject him or her as a person. For example, some Blacks facetiously quote Whites as saying "We've given them the vote. What more do they want?" What "they" want —and what all of us want—is to be accepted as persons, not merely as citizens. All minority ethnic groups are struggling for this ideal today. Thus a society may be democratic in the pure sense of the word, and yet quite destructive of those personal values without which democratic institutions lose all their meaning. Is this fact not borne out in those sections of our country where technical civil rights have never been in question, but where de facto denial of human rights has been widespread?

45

Or do we consider that a technetronic society can be thoroughly democratic by reducing us to I.B.M. numbers?

Observe the crisis of the church. The crucial question which Christians face today is: How can the church enter into the world, make itself truly relevant as an agent of change for the betterment of all people, and yet avoid being swallowed up by the world? It is the same problem faced by the ancient Hebrews, though today it presses in upon us with greater urgency. There are those who are convinced that the church can only become relevant as it ceases to have an institutional form and moves into the world as a "religionless Christianity." These thinkers believe that the old forms of Christianity have become meaningless. However, there are others who believe that it is impossible for the church to fulfill its mission unless it both enters into the world and at the same time maintains a healthy tension between its own existence and the existence of the world. These persons are keenly aware of the many errors of both thought and practice that exist in the life of the church, errors that must be corrected. But they doubt that the new "radical theology," which would abandon the church, is the answer. The church and its theology are never perfected.

Figuratively speaking, we must know that we are "Hebrews" and that we "fear the Lord." But we must hold fast our heritage in the clear knowledge that there is a razor thin edge between a valid pride without which we perish and an unholy pride with which comes our downfall. Nowhere is the crucial doctrine of salvation by faith alone more important than just at this point. Ours is a faith existence which means that we trust not in ourselves that we have arrived, that we are saved, but rather that we are held moment by moment in God's saving grace. St. Paul puts it: ". . . from faith to faith" (*Romans* 1:17, KJV), that is, from one moment of faith to another moment of faith—this is how we live. We do not go from faith to certainty, but "from faith to faith." And yet, this "from faith to faith" is the final and absolute certainty. The very gates of hell cannot prevail against it.

This "from faith to faith" means that we can never possess our faith and build a fence about it. Rather we are possessed by it. We can never settle down and say, "We have it." We can only say, "It has us." The "I am a Hebrew" is both vital and valid. But it is a deadly peril. Around every corner there lurks complacency, self-righteousness and false pride. Without a genuine "and I fear the LORD" it is the virtue that becomes a vice.

Study Questions

1. Today we are continually bombarded with change. Granted the necessity of change, how are we to deal with the constant danger that we will lose the essentials of our heritage? Do we need to begin stressing the things that do not change? If so, what are they?

2. By what standards do we judge our own heritage? Granted that we need the courage to discard old forms, how are we to distinguish that which is good and valid from that which is a block to the fulfillment of God's purpose? Any heritage has three elements:

(1) That which is positive and valid.

(2) That which is negative, a denial of justice and righteousness and a block to progress.

(3) That which is incidental, nonessential.

The extremely difficult question is how to distinguish these elements. Those involved personally in a heritage often see nonessentials as being most essential; evil elements appear as good. In what ways can we seek to overcome this dilemma?

3. Like Jonah we today profess a faith in God and desire to be counted as his children. Are we willing to accept the responsibilities of this privilege? What are the responsibilities of the Christian today?

"Throw Me Into The Sea": Heroics

Then the men were exceedingly afraid, and said to him, "What is this that you have done!" For the men knew that he was fleeing from the presence of the LORD, because he had told them. Then they said to him, "What shall we do to you, that the sea may quiet down for us?" For the sea grew more and more tempestuous. He said to them, "Take me up and throw me into the sea; then the sea will quiet down for you; for I know it is because of me that this great tempest has come upon you." —Jonah 1:10-12

This next episode in the story of Jonah is a further commentary on the dilemma of pride. Indeed, one is amazed at

47

the genius and boldness of the author in laying bare the deepest contradictions of human nature. These contradictions strike at the root of our motive for mission, whether our mission involves crossing salt water or not, whether it is inside the church or outside, whether it is preaching in distant places or proclaiming the gospel on our own street, whether it is working for world peace or struggling for social justice at home.

Our motive for mission must be continually checked and rechecked. There is no occupation that faces the danger of ulterior motives and of both haloes and heroics quite like that of the missionary. Our number one occupational hazard is falling victim to pride and self-righteousness. Jonah appears to have had this problem also. Certainly he was blinded to the truths God was trying to teach him. The lot having fallen upon him, the question arose: What shall be done? Jonah was ready with the answer. Look at the picture the author paints: The storm is raging; the ship is about to sink; crew and passengers will be lost. A brave man steps forward. "Let me die for all of you. Throw me overboard. The storm will cease. You will be spared. I will gladly sacrifice myself." What a hero! J. M. P. Smith comments, "This is the only decent thing Jonah did in the entire story." [12] But wait! Look again a little later in the story. A bitter, sulking man sits on a hill overlooking a great city. "Kill 'em, Lord," he says. "It's your time to act now, Lord. Rain down fire. Blow 'em to bits. What's that, Lord? You mean to say you aren't going to wipe 'em all out? Why you soft-hearted god, you! Now I've lost face! And I hope to die!" (read *Jonah* 4:1-4).

Two different men? No, the same man: Jonah, son of Amittai. Here was a man who in one case was willing to die that the heathen might live. (Or was he? One scholar suggests that he is trying to involve them in his own death, since he himself does not want to take responsibility for it.[13]) In another he had rather die than allow them to live. Actually, however, Jonah was not as inconsistent as he seemed. Both actions—on the ship and in Nineveh—appear to have been motivated by the same thing. It was primarily a matter of pride, of vindicating a claim to superiority. Face must be saved at all cost. In one case it called for heroics; in another for cruelty. One could hardly defend the position that Jonah was actually concerned about the people on the ship. He showed beyond the shadow of a doubt his utter disdain for human life in his attitude toward the Ninevites. Not even helpless children appealed to him. The suggestion that Jonah was concerned about the people on the ship because he was near them and could see their faces, while in the case of Nineveh he was out on a hillside at a distance from the city, overlooks the fact that Jonah had walked through the entire city from one side to the other and had seen the Ninevites face to face.

Jonah's concern, therefore, was not with the travelers. It was with himself, with his own prophetic reputation. He had been caught. His flight from God was the cause of the storm. He must uphold the honor of the superior Hebrew. Nothing ministers to one's pride quite like the call to be a martyr. So Jonah walked up and "took the blame." "Throw me overboard and save the ship." *II Kings* 14:25 indicates that he was a popular national figure in Israel. He, therefore, had a reputation to uphold. Supported no doubt by the leading religious authorities and acclaimed by all the nationalistic organizations as their "hero," he felt compelled to do the "heroic" thing. If this was not Jonah's motive, then it is hard to determine what the motive was since it is clear that he was not really concerned about the people aboard who, so far as we know, were all "heathen." Some of them may even have been Ninevites. The traditional view that Jonah's offering of himself was genuine self-sacrifice is therefore open to serious question. No less a scholar than George Adam Smith makes a great point of Jonah's "conversion" and of his humble self-giving.[14] But Smith's interpretation does not fit the facts of the story and even Smith has difficulty reconciling it with later developments. If Jonah was converted here in chapter one he quickly backslid in chapter four.

But the more serious charge to be leveled against Jonah is that he went on his mission, when he did change his mind and go to Nineveh, primarily because of a desire to vindicate himself and his nation. His chief concern was to destroy the Ninevites and thus to make the world safe for himself and his own vested interests. The church today is suspect in many places in the world of doing the same thing, and who will dispute that many see the Christian mission primarily as an aid to democracy and a tool against communism? Missionaries are accused of having questionable motives. They are often seen either as willing agents or unwitting tools of western economic imperialism. Likewise the church at home and abroad seems at times to be primarily involved in a frantic effort to protect, promote and enhance its own institutional life, instead of being at the forefront of the battle for human rights, giving itself and losing its life for humanity.

In promoting its own health and growth, which, of course, is valid and necessary, the church in any country always runs the danger of becoming an expression of local civil religion and of being unwittingly an instrument of both vested interests and national policy. Certainly this has happened often in the U.S.A when the church has identified itself with American civil religion, has become a heavenly sanctifier of national purpose and has sung lustily "Praise the Lord and pass the ammunition." Even the growing emphasis on ecumenicity has been seen by many as an expression of this dominant concern of the church to save and enhance her own institutional life rather than as a movement into the world in terms of total involvement. We must never lose sight of this danger. Many churches and church councils seek constantly to involve themselves wherever there is human need: distress, oppression, exploitation, denial of human rights and human dignity, strife, conflict. Yet, in spite of the efforts to be the church in the world, hierarchies emerge and institutional interests clamor for attention. We must always be aware of the danger that we may sacrifice the social and evangelistic thrust of the church upon the altar of organizational and institutional harmony.

The day for vested institutionalism and narrow nationalism which seek to protect the status quo is gone. The church must be revolutionary or it will die. Likewise, the day of hypocritical heroics has been exposed as the sham it has always been. A superficial "Throw me into the sea" will not do. We must be genuine, and we must be bold if we are to be true disciples of the most revolutionary character who ever lived—Jesus Christ. Nothing less than the total church in total mission confronting the total world with the total gospel will meet the challenge that confronts us. Ours is both an adequate gospel: the power of God; and a global gospel: to everyone who has faith (Romans 1:16). For haloes and heroics we have no need, but for true heroes of this saving faith every neighborhood in every village and town and city on earth is waiting.

Study Questions

1. What specific dangers of pride do we encounter in our own religious life? in our church? our community?

2. Are there ways in which we use our religion for personal advantage? Why is church membership in a small town considered to be an economic advantage? for a merchant? a lawyer? a doctor? a teacher? other?

3. In what ways do we see the Christian mission as an aid to, and a support for American democracy? Is this valid or not valid? Why? Should the Christian mission be seen as a tool to fight communism? Why?

4. How should missionaries relate to the governments of the countries where they work? Should they support a government even though they know it is corrupt and oppressive? Should they be active politically, engaging in activity designed to bring about change? Should they engage in subversive activity where they are convinced that this is the only way to bring about change in an oppressive, totalitarian regime? Or should they remain neutral and aloof from politics?

"Nevertheless the Men Rowed Hard": Humanization

Nevertheless the men rowed hard to bring the ship back to land, but they could not, for the sea grew more and more tempestuous against them. Therefore they cried to the LORD, "We beseech thee, O LORD, let us not perish for this man's life, and lay not on us innocent blood; for thou, O LORD, hast done as it pleased thee." So they took up Jonah and threw him into the sea; and the sea ceased from its raging. Then the men feared the LORD exceedingly, and they offered a sacrifice to the LORD and made vows.

—Jonah 1:13-16

This event gives the story a new dimension. Even though Jonah urged them to throw him overboard (of course he could have jumped, but this would not have met the ritual requirements of offering a sacrifice), the supposedly cruel, heathen sailors show their large-hearted concern. Earlier they had labored while Jonah slept. Now they choose to risk their own lives in an attempt to save his. They are true heroes. They struggle hard to bring the ship to land to avoid having to throw Jonah overboard. It is entirely possible that some of them hailed from Nineveh. At least they were the hated Góyīm (Gentiles). They were the "lesser breeds without the law."

Then, a little later in the story, this same Hebrew whom the heathen had tried so hard to save, demands the slaughter of a half-million heathen—women, children, and all. One can hardly imagine a more devastating contrast. Is the author suggesting that the heathen sailors are morally superior to a Hebrew prophet? This seems to be his point. But whether he has this contrast specifically in mind or not, it is clear that he intends to place the heathen sailors in a most favorable light by emphasizing their genuine concern for Jonah, just as a little later he places the Ninevites in a favorable light by stressing their instant repentance. There is even an element of loving one's enemies on the part of the heathen sailors. Jonah is the cause of the sailors' trouble, and yet they are trying desperately to save him. As suggested in the exegesis, we are not assuming that their motives were altogether altruistic. Nevertheless, the sailors were genuinely human, and at this point they were allies of Jonah and not enemies.

It has taken Christians a long time to get out of their shell of exclusivism and to recognize the fact that adherents of other faiths may be allies and not enemies. Yet the acceptance of persons of other faiths as allies raises a crucial issue. As long as we had neat categories of God's people and the devil's people, we could generate enthusiasm for our rescue missions to "heathen lands." We could send Jonahs out to Nineveh. But today the world is shrinking into one vast neighborhood. The Ninevehs are no longer out there, but on our own shores. Having met people of other faiths, having observed much nobility among them and having studied some of the beautiful tenets of their faiths, can we still justify missions? If Nineveh is not all bad and Israel is not all good, why should we go as missionaries? Is not the world mission of the Christian church null and void?

Not at all! We have always insisted that we should preach Christ to the so-called "Christian" world. The only basic change in attitude is the recognition that we share a common humanity with all cultures and all religions. This change of attitude in no way alters the fact that all persons need the gospel, all persons need Christ. We need the gospel because in the gospel God speaks. The revelation in Christ is God speaking to the world and not the world speaking to itself in a loud voice.[15] God speaks in Jesus Christ not only of himself, but also of his creation. And he speaks to *all*. As the God-man, Jesus Christ reveals both true Godhead and true humanity. Such revelation is not merely propositional, that is, only a disclosure of facts. It is existential. It opens a new mode of existence, the new creation in Christ. It opens up new possibilities of genuine humanization. Comparing one religion with another (Christianity included) actually means comparing one culture with another, which always ends in cultural pride. It is, however, an entirely different thing for Christians to join hands with people of all races and cultures and religions in a common humanity to say, "Let us all come, Christians and non-Christians alike, to the foot of the cross." [16] This, we believe, is the heart of true evangelism. D. T. Niles, the outstanding Asian theologian of our generation, is reported to have said, "Evangelism is one beggar telling another beggar where to find bread." Evangelism has nothing to do with religious labels.

"Nevertheless the men rowed hard." The least Jonah could have done was to have picked up an oar and helped them! It was his life they were trying to save.

Study Questions

1. Are there persons of a religious faith other than Christian in your neighborhood? Have you gone out of your way to know them? Have you learned to appreciate their religious and cultural heritage? How can you learn from them? How would you present Christ to them?

2. Is it necessary for one to change religious labels in order to become a Christian? What is involved in becoming a Christian? Where do baptism and church affiliation fit in? Some today are speaking of anonymous Christians and of the unknown Christ or hidden Christ in all cultures and religions. Is this a valid concept? Discuss the pros and cons.

3. Can other religions be allies of Christianity? How?

4. In what ways can Christian churches in my community join together for a more effective witness?

5. One proposal for ecumenical witness is that of COCU (Consultation on Church Union). Discuss this plan, looking at the pros and cons.

Exegesis

1:5. *The mariners:* Sailors from different tribes or nations as is shown by the fact that they worshipped different gods. An interesting thought is that some of them may have been from Nineveh, with their families still back in the city.

Cried to his own god: Each sailor looked to the god of his own tribe or locality for protection. In a crisis he forgot that his god's power had territorial limitations.

Wares: Probably included some of the cargo and also the part of the ship's tackle and equipment that was not absolutely essential. *The Interpreter's Bible* and other commentaries interpret this verse in terms of lightening the ship (a common practice in a storm) which would cause it to ride higher in the water and thus be less likely to be swamped by the high waves. However, the Hebrew construction indicates that it was the sea which was to be "lightened"—that is, appeased by the sacrificial offering of the "wares." (We still use the expression, a "heavy sea.") The Hebrew actually says "lighten upon them," or "make it easier for them." When the offering of wares was insufficient to appease the storm, the sailors decided a further sacrifice must be made (vss. 11-12).

Fast asleep: There have been many theories as to why Jonah went to sleep: he was exhausted running from God; he had a troubled conscience and was trying to forget his disobedience; being away from Israel and thus no longer under Yahweh's jurisdiction, he could rest in peace; he had peace of mind because in spite of his disobedience, he was still a prophet and thus was under Yahweh's special protection; he had had a hard day getting to Joppa and was worn out; and of course there is always the possibility he was seasick. Whatever the reason for his drowsiness, Jonah found the ship comfortable, quiet and conducive to sleep, as all know who have traveled by ocean liner. There have been attempts to compare Jonah's sleep with that of Jesus in the midst of the storm (*Mark* 4:35-49). But the parallel hardly seems appropriate. Jesus was asleep because of a deep inner peace resulting from an at-one-ness with the Father. If Jonah was asleep because of his faith, then he was a master of self-deception. It is clear that there was no at-one-ness between Yahweh and Jonah. Rather, they were at war with each other, and the battle of wills was fought to the bitter end in chapter four.

1:6. *Captain*: Shipmaster, literally "master of the ropes." Compare *Ezekiel* 27:8, 27, 29 which use the word *pilot* for virtually the same Hebrew expression.

You sleeper: The captain is amazed to find Jonah asleep. Whether he is angry with Jonah or only amazed that he can sleep in such a crisis is not clear. But whatever the tone of voice, the captain shouts, "Get up you fool and start praying."

Your god: The RSV rightly spells god with a small "g." The ship captain's action in arousing Jonah does not indicate that he considers Jonah's god any more powerful or any more important than any other. The captain is clearly a polytheist, believing that there are many gods. He does not know for sure who Jonah is or who his god is, but in time of crisis everyone must pray. Perhaps it is precisely this sleeper's god who is angry and needs placating. Or perhaps this particular god could help if asked. The author no doubt intends a sharp barb of irony in that it is a pagan ship captain who must prod a Hebrew prophet to pray.

1:7. *Cast lots*: The use of some scheme of chance in determining guilt or in discerning the will of deity was quite common in ancient times. The belief was that the deity would influence the results and thus would make his will known. *Proverbs* 16:33 says, "The lot is cast into the lap, but the decision is wholly from the LORD." In *I Samuel* 10:20-24 Saul is chosen king by lot. Samuel thus calls Saul, "him whom the LORD has chosen." In *Acts* 1:26 Matthias is chosen by lot to take the place of Judas. (It will be noted, however, that this method is not used again in the New Testament.) *Numbers* 26:53-56 specifies that land shall be divided to the tribes of Israel by lot. *Joshua* 7:14-21 describes the apprehending of a culprit by lot, and *I Samuel* 14:40-42 shows how guilt is determined by lot. The decision of the lot was regarded as authoritative and final because it was considered God's decision.

The lot fell upon Jonah: The author further elaborates his theme of the impossibility of escaping God. First, the angry storm points a finger at the ship. Now the casting of lots points a finger at Jonah: "Thou art the man!"

On whose account: The lot had already shown who was guilty, so the question is redundant. Possibly the sailors wanted confirmation in the form of a personal confession. Or possibly the author includes the question for purposes of emphasis. However, it should also be noted that the Septuagint and several Hebrew manuscripts omit the question, and it may not have been in the original.

1:8. *What is your occupation?* The sailors have no idea what Jonah's occupation is. Possibly it is one that is offensive to the god causing the storm. How embarrassing for Jonah to have to admit that he is a prophet! (And note that he never does admit it.) A prophet running from God! A prophet asleep in time of crisis! Also the question does not relate merely to Jonah's occupation or profession, but inquires: What is your business or your purpose in making this trip? No wonder Jonah does not answer the question.

Whence do you come? In asking questions about who Jonah is, where he is from and to what people he belongs, the sailors are trying to probe further the possible cause of the storm. The staccato with which the questions pour forth reveals the panic that had seized them.

1:9. *I am a Hebrew:* The sailors ask Jonah five questions. He replies to only one, the question of nationality. The term *Hebrew* was used by the Israelites when speaking with foreigners about themselves. Observe *Exodus* 2:7 where Miriam is speaking with the Egyptian princess and *Genesis* 40:15 where Joseph is speaking with the Egyptian butler.

I fear the LORD: "Fear" is used not in the sense of fright, but in the sense of reverence, worship or standing in awe of. The sailors do not ask Jonah about his religion, but he is on the defensive. He knows that he is defying God; hence he must deny it by declaring that he reverences God.

The God of heaven: A quite common way of designating Yahweh in the post-exilic period, although the same expression was also used before the exile (see Genesis 24:7). Compare *Ezra* 1:2 and passages throughout the book of *Ezra;* also *Nehemiah* 1:4 and *Daniel* 2:18, 19, 37.

Who made the sea and the dry land: Jonah is aware that some of the Phoenician sailors probably worship Ba'al Shamem, which means "the Lord of heaven." He therefore adds the phrase, "who made the sea and the dry land." The incongruity between his theoretical position—his knowledge that he cannot escape God—and his actual practice in running from God seems not to be apparent to him at this time. But the author in making this inconsistency clear in the first chapter lays the groundwork for the climax in chapter four.

1:10. *The men were exceedingly afraid:* A storm at sea is always a frightful thing. But in this case the fear of the sailors is increased by the knowledge that they have on board a fugitive from the god who has made the sea. No wonder this god is angry! He may even increase the fury of the storm, and they will all be lost.

What is this that you have done!: This is half question, half exclamation. The sailors are saying, "What do you mean coming aboard our ship and endangering all of our lives!"

For the men knew that he was fleeing. This verse is somewhat awkward in that the author after describing the great fear of the sailors suddenly realizes that up to this point they have had no way of knowing that Jonah is a fugitive from Yahweh. So he adds by way of parenthesis, "For the men knew that he was fleeing from the presence of the Lord, because he told them." Even then, the sailors do not know the reason for the flight. They probably conclude that he is a criminal seeking to escape punishment. They do not press him, and he does not reveal to them the reason for his flight.

1:11. *What shall we do to you?* The sailors are honestly puzzled. Something has to be done quickly, but what? If the angry deity were one of their own gods, they would know what to do to appease him, but for the Hebrew's god they are uncertain. Also, not knowing the exact nature of Jonah's offense they are unsure of the kind of recompense demanded. They cannot afford to make a mistake because their lives are at stake; so they ask Jonah to tell them what will appease his god. Jonah has two choices: ask the sailors to return him to land or risk death in the ocean. He chooses the latter, since he would rather die than carry out God's mission. (See chapter V, section 1.)

1:12. *Take me up and throw me into the sea:* In ancient times it was generally believed that the wrath of a god causing a storm at sea could be appeased either by throwing the offending party overboard or by setting him adrift in a small boat. There is a parallel to this account in Indian tradition. Mittavindaka, son of a merchant of Benares, goes to sea in disobedience to the command of his mother. The ship suddenly stops at sea and will not go until Mittavindaka (selected by lot as Jonah had been) is set adrift in a small boat. The ship then proceeds on its way. Babylonian, Egyptian and Greek traditions have similar stories.[17]

1:13. *The men rowed hard:* Literally, "dug" or "ploughed" the sea. Ordinarily sailors prefer to ride out a storm at sea rather than to risk being dashed onto a rocky shore. However, in this case they decide to try to make it back to port in order to get Jonah off the ship. Of course they are concerned about themselves, but they also seem genuinely concerned about Jonah. With their sails destroyed and useless, the only recourse is to row.

1:14. *Let us not perish for this man's life.* When it becomes clear that the ship cannot make it to port, the sailors decide to throw Jonah overboard. But first they offer a prayer to Yahweh. Some have supposed that the offering of a prayer indicates a sudden special reverence for Yahweh. Patterson even speaks of repentance.[18] But this appears to be a complete misunderstanding of what was taking place. The sailors assume quite naturally that they are throwing Jonah to his death. Suppose he is innocent. They have nothing against him personally. Or suppose Yahweh acts arbitrarily and takes his own worshipper's side against them. They want to make it clear that the responsibility is on Yahweh. It is Yahweh who has sent the storm; Yahweh has caused the lot to fall on Jonah; and Yahweh has prevented the ship's return to land. Now it is Yahweh who directs the sailors to throw Jonah overboard: "thou, O LORD, hast done as it pleased thee." There is here the subtle suggestion that the heathen sailors are actually agents of God in turning Jonah back and in sending him on his mission.

Innocent blood: The sailors are not indicating that they think Jonah is innocent. They do not know what he has or has not done. But they want it clear that, if he is innocent, the blame for throwing an innocent man overboard rests upon Yahweh and not upon them.

Ceased from its raging: The sea is pictured as animate. It has been angry. Now it is appeased and calm.

1:16. *The men feared the Lord:* The sailors are greatly impressed by the sudden calm. The traditional view has held that the sailors were converted to Yahweh.[19] However, there is no hint that they embrace the Hebrew faith or that they become worshippers of Yahweh. In a polytheistic society one shows no disloyalty to his own god when he offers a sacrifice to another. The sailors want both to express thanksgiving and also to receive Yahweh's further goodwill. What kind of vows they make the author does not say. Probably they promise certain gifts once the ship reaches port. Nothing more is heard of the sailors.

Footnotes

[1] Halford E. Luccock, *Marching off the Map* (New York: Harper and Brothers, 1952), p. 129.

[2] Quoted as a Foreword in Chester Bowles, *New Dimensions of Peace* (New York: Harper and Brothers, 1955).

[3] Aldous Huxley in *Science, Liberty and Peace* (New York: Harper and Brothers, 1946). pp. 42 ff.

[4] J. B. Phillips, *Your God Is Too Small* (New York: The MacMillan Co., 1954), p. 58.

[5] Eugene Smith, *God's Mission and Ours* (New York: Abingdon, 1961), p. 109.

[6] From a letter in the *Memphis Commercial Appeal*, quoted in *Newsweek*, November 5, 1962.

[7] Arnold Toynbee, *The World and the West* (New York: Oxford University Press, 1953), p. 85.

[8] K. M. Panikkar, *Asia and Western Dominance* (London: George Allen and Unwin, Ltd., 1955), p. 507.

[9] *Ibid.*

[10] William J. Ledderer and Eugene Burdick, *The Ugly American* (New York: W. W. Norton and Co., Inc., 1958).

[11] November 1963. The occasion was attended by the author.

[12] J. M. P. Smith, *The Prophets and Their Times* (Chicago: University of Chicago Press, 1915), p. 223.

[13] George M. Landes, in unpublished correspondence with the author.

[14] George Adam Smith, *The Book of the Twelve Prophets* (New York: George H. Doran Co., n. d.), II, pp. 507 ff.

[15] See Karl Barth, *Church Dogmatics, A Selection* (New York: Harper Torchbooks, 1961), pp. 87-133.

[16] Observe the emphasis of Hendrik Kraemer at this point. See *The Christian Message in a Non-Christian World* (New York: Harper and Brothers, 1938).

[17] See Julius Bewer, *et al.*, *A Critical and Exegetical Commentary on Haggai, Zechariah, Malachi and Jonah*, one of the volumes of the *International Critical Commentary*, edited by Charles A. Briggs, *et al.* (New York: Charles Scribner's Sons, 1912), Section on *Jonah*, p. 35; Charles Foster Kent, *The Sermons, Epistles and Apocalypses of Israel's Prophets* (New York: Charles Scribner's Sons, 1910), p. 420; Frederick Carl Eiselen, *The Minor Prophets* (New York: Eaton and Mains, 1907), p. 339.

[18] John Patterson, *The Goodly Fellowship of the Prophets* (New York: Charles Scribner's Sons, 1948), p. 277.

[19] Jacob Myers, *Hosea to Jonah* (London: S.C.M. Press, 1959), p. 167.

IV
REPENTANCE

"And It Vomited Out Jonah": Second Chance

And the LORD appointed a great fish to swallow up
Jonah; and Jonah was in the belly of the fish three days
and three nights.

Then Jonah prayed to the LORD his God from the belly
of the fish, saying,

> "I called to the LORD, out of my distress,
>> and he answered me;
>
> Out of the belly of Sheol I cried,
>> and thou didst hear my voice.
>
> For thou didst cast me into the deep,
>> into the heart of the seas,
>>> and the flood was round about me;
>>> all thy waves and thy billows passed over me.
>>> Then I said, 'I am cast out from thy presence;
> how shall I look upon thy holy temple?'
>> The waters closed in over me,
>>> the deep was round about me;
>> weeds were wrapped about my head
>>> at the roots of the mountains.
>> I went down to the land
>>> whose bars closed upon me forever;
>> yet thou didst bring up my life from the Pit,
>>> O LORD my God.
>> When my soul fainted within me,
>>> I remembered the LORD;
>> and my prayer came to thee,
>>> into thy holy temple.
>> Those who pay regard to vain idols
>>> forsake their true loyalty,

> But I with the voice of thanksgiving
> will sacrifice to thee;
> what I have vowed I will pay.
> Deliverance belongs to the LORD."
> And the LORD spoke to the fish, and it vomited out
> Jonah upon the dry land. —Jonah 1:17-2:10

As noted in the last chapter, the heathen sailors labored heroically to save Jonah. Only when the storm proved too much for the ship did they consent to throw him overboard. Was Jonah grateful for their deep concern? Hardly. A short time later he proved himself so completely ungrateful and so completely self-centered that his own pride and his own comfort meant more to him than the plight of a half-million people. Yet, in his own eyes, he was a true prophet of God!

The amazing thing, however, is that God did use Jonah! In this we can all take hope. God did provide the fish. The fish did vomit Jonah out on dry land. Whether he vomited Jonah out because of nausea or because of God's purpose, or both, God did give Jonah a second chance. God's patience is beyond human comprehension and his use of even the most unworthy servant is astounding. *Psalms 76:10* declares: "Surely the wrath of men shall praise thee."

We come now to consider the way in which God did use Jonah in Nineveh. We will see how Jonah's wrath (In 4:9 Jonah says he is angry enough to die!) is turned to the glory of God. But first, we must see how Jonah perverted his mission and sought to use it as an opportunity to bring about the destruction of his hated enemies, the Ninevites.

Study Questions

1. Some critics of the church claim that it, like Jonah, is proud, arrogant, smug, self-righteous. Can we be big enough to take our critics seriously? How can they help us? Why is there so much antagonism to the church and to organized religion today?

2. How is God using the church in your community in spite of its shortcomings? Be specific.

3. What are the things that you dislike most about the church today?

4. Is your church a concerned church? For whom? On what does it spend most of its money?

5. Is the church in your community in any way like Jonah?

"Nineveh Shall Be Overthrown": Saving Sinners

Then the word of the LORD came to Jonah the second time, saying, "Arise, go to Nineveh, that great city, and proclaim to it the message that I tell you." So Jonah arose and went to Nineveh, according to the word of the LORD. Now Nineveh was an exceedingly great city, three days' journey in breadth. Jonah began to go into the city, going a day's journey. And he cried, "Yet forty days, and Nineveh shall be overthrown!" —Jonah 3:1-4

Jonah's mission was to save the Ninevites. He perverted it into a mission to destroy them. They were the hated enemies of Israel, as we have already observed. Now was his chance. There is something in human nature that seems to find a devilish delight in denouncing others. It gets a satanic satisfaction out of consigning people to torment. The solemn tone of Jonah's voice but thinly disguised the note of enjoyment with which he uttered his dire warning.

Jonah received at least three subtle psychological satisfactions out of condemning the Ninevites: first, a feeling of importance; second a release of pent-up emotions, an outlet for sadistic feelings under the pious guise of preaching; and third, a sense of power in using God to achieve his own purposes. In short, Jonah was delighted to play the role of God. With great gusto he thundered forth God's judgment on Nineveh. How human nature loves this Jonah approach! How we love to play the role of God. What deep satisfaction we experience when we declare God's wrath upon the children of disobedience. How pleasant are the subtle satisfactions of saving sinners! What a sense of importance comes to us when we are on the judging end of judgment!

In direct contrast to the Jonah approach is the Christlike approach. They who follow the Jonah approach major on condemnation; they who follow the Christlike approach major on commendation: commendation of the love of God. They commend not a soft, sentimental love, but a love that purges and purifies. They point to the "expulsive power of a new affection." [1] They come in humility, in repentance, in appreciation of the good and in sincere agonizing over the evil. They seek to understand, to share, to point ever to Christ, knowing that we all stand together under the judgment of God, under the sign of Jonah. They who follow the Christlike approach see the agony in the human situation in which we are all involved. They know that there are no simple answers to our dilemma. They know the deep anguish of having to compromise, of having to do less than they would like, in order that they might do more than deliver their souls and then run away to sit on a hill and watch Nineveh burn.

Contrast Jonah sitting on a hill overlooking Nineveh with Jesus sitting on a hill overlooking Jerusalem. Jonah was saying, "Destroy the city, Lord!" Jesus, with great pathos in his voice, was saying, "O Jerusalem, Jerusalem . . . How often would I have gathered your children together as a hen gathers her brood under her wings, and you would not!" (*Matthew* 23:37). How easy it would have been for Jesus to proclaim his message, deliver his soul, clear his conscience and, like Jonah, move on. But he loved too deeply for that.

So today there are prophets who choose the hard way. They could make a bold witness, declare unequivocal convictions, deliver unmistakable condemnations—and then move on to the comfort of a booth or a gourd vine. This would be easy. But they choose the hard way: they choose to stay. Unlike Jonah, they know that they too stand under the judgment of God. If Nineveh goes, they will go, too. If God's wrath strikes, they will be at point zero, not out on a hill piously looking on. Their way is a heartbreaking way, for they as individuals must live with the haunting questions: "Have I been silent when I should have been outspoken? Have I soft-pedaled in the name of discretion? Have I betrayed under the guise of strategy?"

Such prophets enjoy no selfish satisfactions in their efforts to save sinners. Theirs is the lonely road of the cross. Theirs is a true calvary. They stand with no supporting group that calls them heroes and sends them on a march to Nineveh to declare their corporate convictions. As they struggle to make their witness, they carry in their breast that awful, haunting fear that they may compromise convictions out of cowardice, or be controlled unconsciously by self-interest. This is the tension they must live under. This is the way of the cross. Compared to those who have the easy road and the sweet satisfaction of marching forth to make a clear witness, their lot is an agonizing Gethsemane.

For the way of the cross is never an easy way. Often the greatest agony is experienced when the way of the cross cuts squarely across the way of kind and good people who are so wonderful, yet so blind to the incongruities between their way and the way of the cross. The fact is that all of us at one time or another fit into this category. Jonah was perfectly sure that the Ninevites were the problem and that he was the solution. But God's real problem—the problem he was desperately trying to deal with—was Jonah.

And so with us. In our self-righteousness (whether pious or worldly), we always think we are the solution, but in fact we are always the problem. Always we want to cry God's judgment on the children of disobedience. Always we see ourselves as saints and others as sinners. Always we want to march in, declare God's judgment on the sinners and then stand off on a hillside or sit under a gourd vine while Nineveh burns. And always the book of *Jonah* protests our pitiful performance.

Study Questions

1. Describe the satisfactions which Jonah received out of condemning the Ninevites.

2. In what ways do we follow what the author calls the "Jonah approach" rather than the "Christlike" approach?

3. If we take the "Christlike" approach can we speak out clearly on unpopular issues without alienating ourselves from our community? How?

4. When Christians have sincere differences of opinion on crucial, sensitive issues, how should they relate to each other? Can we disagree deeply and still love each other and maintain fellowship?

5. What is the most effective way to witness against entrenched evils in society: the indirect approach or the head-on approach?

6. Can one bring a message of judgment and do it in love? How?

7. Which causes a person more suffering: to speak out on one's moral convictions and alienate oneself, or to compromise and suffer qualms of conscience?

"Let Everyone Turn": Repentance

And the people of Nineveh believed God; they proclaimed a fast, and put on sackcloth, from the greatest of them to the least of them. Then tidings reached the king of Nineveh, and he arose from his throne, removed his robe, and covered himself with sackcloth, and sat in ashes. And he made proclamation and published through Nineveh, "By the decree of the king and his nobles: Let neither man nor beast, herd nor flock, taste anything; let them not feed, or drink water, but let man and beast be covered with sackcloth, and let them cry mightily to God; yea, let everyone turn from his evil way and from the violence which is in his hands. Who knows, God may yet repent and turn from his fierce anger, so that we perish not?" —Jonah 3:5-9

Jonah finally went to Nineveh because he hoped thereby to cause its destruction. Perhaps the ferocious storm had convinced him that God was angry enough to destroy the Ninevites. Jonah knew through personal experience that God could be stern in judgment. However, an amazing thing happened. Contrary to his ardent wishes, the Ninevites actually listened to him and repented. One of the major facets of the book of *Jonah* is its depiction of the ready response of the Ninevites to the "word of the LORD." The author stresses the fact that the so-called heathen are not bad people who should be destroyed, but are the object of God's loving mercy. When the word is proclaimed, they respond immediately. Note also that they respond not to an institution or a "mission" or a movement, but to God. Too often we have equated response to Christ with response to our mission or our church. We are finally learning that Christ is not confined to our western institutions and response to him is free and open and may take many forms. So thorough and genuine is Nineveh's repentance that it becomes a model to which Jesus refers several centuries later. In *Luke* 11:29-32 Jesus says: "This generation is an evil generation; it seeks a sign, but no sign shall be given to it except the sign of Jonah. . . . The men of Nineveh will arise at the judgment with this generation and condemn it; for they repented at the preaching of Jonah, and behold, something greater than Jonah is here."

This incident in which Jesus uses the expression, the "sign of Jonah," is also recorded in *Matthew* 12:38-42 and 16:1-4. *Mark* 8:11-12 relates the incident but does not mention Jonah: "Why does this generation seek a sign? Truly, I say to you, no sign shall be given to this generation." All four passages are set in the context of Jesus' demand for repentance, as is apparent in the verses from *Luke* quoted above. The "sign of Jonah" was both the repentance of the Ninevites and also the need of Jonah for repentance since God's judgment was actually more upon Jonah than upon Nineveh. There is a kind of play on words here. Jesus was setting the "sign of Jonah" over against a "sign." He was suggesting that the Jews should submit to internal cleansing through repentance (the sign of Jonah) rather than seeking an external miracle (a sign).

All four of the passages referred to above use the phrase, "No sign shall be given." Jesus was saying to his hearers: You will receive no miraculous sign to authenticate the Word which stands before you, for no sign can authenticate God's self-authenticating Word. You can only accept or reject. Remember, the people of Nineveh received no sign. They had only the proclaimed word. Yet, they believed and repented. The same demand is upon you. The revelation that needs no sign stands before you. The appropriate response is not a demand that you be convinced by a sign, but a willingness to be convicted of sin. For you to demand a sign is to set yourselves up as judge, when the fact is that you are being judged.

In the New Testament reference to Jonah, *Matthew* 12:40 suggests a parallelism between Jonah's three days and three nights in the fish and the time Jesus spent in the tomb.[2] Actually, the parallelism is only approximate since Jesus was in the tomb only two nights and a part of three days. Also the Gospels make clear that Jesus' major purpose was to stress repentance. A careful reading of the *Matthew* account beginning with 12:33 will leave one in no doubt that repentance is the central focus. All four passages where the theme is mentioned stress repentance while only one verse in one of the four mentions the resurrection. Likewise it should be noted that

Matthew 12:40 actually suggests a miraculous sign, whereas the basic point of all four passages is that "no sign shall be given." Some have suggested that 12:40 may be a later interpolation, since the passage, omitting verse 40, is a simple discourse on repentance and is more coherent. In any event, it seems clear that the expression, "the sign of Jonah," in all of the passages where it appears refers basically to the demand for repentance. We therefore view it in this way.

Returning to the book of *Jonah* itself, we observe further the place of repentance in the plan of salvation. Contrast for a moment verse 3:8 with verse 1:9: "let everyone turn from his evil way" (3:8) expresses humble repentance; "I am a Hebrew" (1:9) expresses just the opposite. These two verses represent two views of salvation. The Ninevites were humble and repentant, trusting only in God's mercy. Jonah, on the other hand, was proud and unrepentant. He was a Hebrew, a member of God's chosen people. Indeed, the entire book may be viewed as a contrast between Israel and Nineveh. Jonah represents Israel's concept of salvation by heritage: "We have Abraham to our fathers." Nineveh, on the other hand, represents salvation by humility. Nineveh is not saved because it is good. Rather it is saved precisely because it recognizes that it is bad. The audacious teaching of the book of *Jonah* at this point is not only that the Gentiles are saved when they repent, but more specifically that they are an example for the Israelites. This was indeed revolutionary. The Israelites thought they were the example (the chosen) for all the world to emulate.

One of the most profound challenges with which Christianity confronts society today is the demand of the gospel for repentance. The mood of the majority today seems to be the mood of Jonah, not the mood of Nineveh. We do not want to hear about sin and repentance. We want to celebrate our humanity, our secularity, our self-sufficiency, and our role as masters of the world around us. The existential anxiety and the recognition of sinfulness so dominant in the fifties and early sixties are gone. The center of the theological stage has again shifted from the sovereignty of God to human action—to a new kind of humanism. In recent consultations with Christians and with persons of other faiths, it has appeared to this writer that the Christian doctrine of sin, of repentance and of justification by faith alone are not acceptable.

There is much to be said for the current emphasis that sounds anew the note of joy and optimism. We must not underestimate our possibilities nor remove our responsibility by an over-emphasis on the sovereignty of God. But there are indications that the new humanism may not be much more realistic than the older liberalism. A naive view of human nature can only end in disillusionment. Facts are facts. Sin is not abolished by wishing it so. Nineveh is still with us, and so is Jonah. We still confront a world torn by strife, filled with hate and dominated by selfishness. Wars continue; the crime rate soars; homes are broken; children suffer; cruel systems crush persons' lives, rob them of dignity, and consign them to a meaningless limbo. Economic injustice and racial bigotry do not yield as easily as we once thought to idealistic demonstrations against them. There is the demonic element in humanity, and only those completely out of touch with reality can ignore it.

Only a theology that shouts "Repent!" has any adequate grasp of the human dilemma. Anything short of this is only a superficial face-lifting. It is like cutting off the surface of a cancer. The roots remain and the infection spreads. The only hope is in digging out the roots. Salvation is in repentance, in cleansing, in a new humanity. It is a most significant fact that the Jewish people read the book of *Jonah* on their Day of Atonement. Our only hope is in atonement—in "at-one-ment" between us and God, between us and others. For in this hope is embodied the new creation in Christ. Paradoxical though it may seem, the hope of the new creation is only born when all human hope is gone. The possibilities open when our shallow self-confidence is shattered. The sun dawns on the eastern horizon following the dark night of despair when, at long last, we stand in abject surrender under the "sign of Jonah." No longer are we sitting on a hill (or in a cloistered sanctuary) in self-sufficiency and self-righteous judgment. We are down in Nineveh on our knees.

Have we reached this place today? If we have there is hope. A theology of hope that will not end in despair must be hammered out in Nineveh, and the theologians might consider sackcloth and ashes for the new clerical garb. The church's going into the world cannot stop short of Nineveh. If it does, the words *relevance, renewal* and *revolution* will turn out to be mere shibboleths. On the other hand, if we are truly willing to go down on our knees together under the sign of Jonah, then the greatest hour of the Christian church can be just ahead.

Study Questions

1. Contrast Jonah's concept of salvation through heritage with Nineveh's understanding of salvation through humility.

2. Do you see signs of repentance in America today? in your own church? Be specific.

3. Is repentance necessary for salvation? If so, why? What do we mean by salvation by faith alone?

4. In January of 1973 a conference met in Bangkok, Thailand, under the auspices of the World Council of Churches to explore the meaning of salvation today. The conference posed three questions: (1) By what criteria can Christians assess the manifold ways in which salvation is experienced as true expressions of God's varied grace? (2) How far do the struggles and expectations of men and women today relate to the gospel of salvation? (3) What is the relationship between saving faith and response through obedience in concrete situations today? How would you answer these questions in the light of your study of Jonah?

5. In terms of both personal and social salvation, what does salvation mean for you? for the victim of political and economic oppression in Latin America? for the man with hungry children in Bangladesh? for the victim of racial discrimination and oppression in Rhodesia? for the Black in the U.S.A. who is denied full personhood and full civil rights—who is looked down upon by many whites as a "nigger"?

6. Nineveh was "wicked" and Jonah was "righteous." Which needed most to repent? Which is harder to repent of: moral wickedness or spiritual pride?

Exegesis

1:17. *The LORD appointed a great fish:* The kind of fish is not specified. E. B. Pusey surmises on the basis of certain maritime stories that it was a white shark (*squalus carcharias*). He points to a number of illustrations such as an incident reported in 1768 in which a sailor fell overboard and was allegedly swallowed by a twenty-foot shark. The shark was shot and immediately discharged the sailor into the water unhurt. The shark was later displayed in Erlangen, Nurnberg and other places.[3] Other scholars have made various suggestions, some surmising that the "big fish" was a sperm whale. But the text of Jonah only says that it was a "large fish," and this is all we know.

Three days and three nights: Matthew 12:40 relates this expression to the time Jesus spent in the tomb. Hosea 6:2 mentions three days as a period of judgment upon Israel, after which she shall be delivered.[4]

2:1. *Jonah prayed:* The reader naturally expects this prayer to be a frantic appeal for help, but to his amazement he finds that it is a prayer of thanksgiving. Nowhere is there any suggestion that the one praying is in the belly of a fish. The picture is of one who has almost drowned in the bottom of the sea, but is now rescued. There is not the slightest appeal for help. There is no expression of regret for disobedience, and the promise at the end is rather perfunctory. The nature of the prayer has been explained in various ways: (1) It is a prayer spoken by Jonah after he was vomited out by the fish, in which case it should properly come after verse 2:10. (2) It is a psalm of thanksgiving uttered in the fish's belly when Jonah suddenly discovers that he is safe from the raging sea. He expresses thanksgiving for full deliverance even before it comes, because his faith assures him it will come. (3) It is a psalm inserted at this point in the story by a later writer who saw its resemblance to the experience of Jonah. For some time most twentieth century scholarship has been inclined toward this view. (4) It is a psalm of praise celebrating deliverance from distress. The author of *Jonah* uses it because it fits into his theme. George Landes argues effectively that the original author, not a later writer, inserted the psalm.[5] This fourth alternative seems more likely to the present writer.

Out of my distress: Note the parallel to *Psalms* 18:6 and 120:1.

2:2 *Belly of Sheol:* Sheol in the Old Testament is the shadowy abode of the dead. It is not the same as hell, which is a concept that entered Jewish thought quite late. Sheol is sometimes personified as a monster with a belly (see *Isaiah* 5:14 where Sheol's large mouth and large appetite are spoken of). Since Jonah is in the belly of the fish when he says "out of the belly of Sheol I cried," it seems logical to equate "belly of the fish" with "belly of Sheol." Some scholars question this identification, however, since the Hebrew word translated "belly" is in each case different. They prefer to connect "belly of Sheol" with the "deep" of verse 3 rather than the "belly of the fish." Possibly the author of *Jonah* in selecting the psalm saw both aspects. However, verses 3, 5 and 6 stress the sea, which likely indicates that this was uppermost in his mind.

2:3. *Heart of the seas:* One of the chief characteristics of Hebrew poetry is this use of parallelism. Being swallowed up in the "heart of the seas" is equivalent to being in the "belly of Sheol"!

All thy waves and thy billows passed over me: The same phrase is found in *Psalms* 42:7.

2:4. *Cast out from thy presence:* Closely parallel to *Psalms* 31:22.

How shall I again look upon thy temple? From the time of Josiah (621 B.C.), worship was centralized in the temple at Jerusalem, and the temple became increasingly dear to the Israelites. During the exile in Babylon they missed the temple more than anything else: "By the waters of Babylon there we sat down and wept when we remembered Zion . . . How shall we sing the Lord's song in a foreign land?" The Babylonian tormentors had commanded: "Sing us one of the songs of Zion!" (*Psalms* 137:1-6).

2:5. *Waters closed in over me:* See *Lamentations* 3:54; *Psalms* 18:4, 69:1-2.

Weeds: Seaweed. The metaphor here is the bottom of the ocean and not the belly of a fish. It is the analogy of a person drowning.

2:6. *At the roots of the mountains:* Means "deep in the sea." It is a reflection of an ancient Hebrew idea that the earth was floating on water. *Psalms* 24:2 says that God has "founded it [the earth] upon the seas and established it upon the rivers."

I went down to the land where bars closed upon me: The metaphor shifts from the sea back to the earth or, to be more specific, to the land under the earth. Sheol (down inside the earth) has "bars" or "gates" that close upon one who enters. It is the land of no return. See *Isaiah* 38:10; *Job* 17:16; 38:17; *Psalms* 9:13; *Matthew* 16:18 KJV.

Thou didst bring up my life from the pit: An echo of *Psalms* 30:3. *Pit* usually refers to the grave or to Sheol.

2:7. *My prayer came to thee, into thy holy temple:* Physical separation from Yahweh and the temple did not prevent prayers from reaching the temple. See *Psalms* 18:6.

2:8. *Those who pay regard to vain idols:* A reference to those who were guilty of apostasy. The same words are used in *Psalms* 31:6. See *Deuteronomy* 32:21.

Forsake their true loyalty: Some translations read "forsake their own mercy"—that is, forsake Yahweh, the source of mercy.

2:9. *Voice of thanksgiving:* The psalm ends with a note of thanksgiving and a promise to fulfill one's vow to God. There is a firm affirmation that God is the only source of salvation. See *Psalms* 3:8 and 50:14-15.

2:10. *The Lord spoke:* Again the emphasis is on God's action through his speaking.

Vomited out Jonah: See pages 24 ff. for a discussion of the relationship between this expression and the description of the exile in *Jeremiah* 51:34, 44.

Dry land: The place is not specified. It was no doubt along the eastern coast of the Mediterranean, and may have been near Joppa where Jonah set sail. Tradition, however, has put the site near Sidon on the Phoenician coast north of Joppa, the assumption being that the fish as an agent of God would carry Jonah in the direction of Nineveh.

3:3. *Jonah arose and went:* This verse has been interpreted to mean that Jonah obeyed God. He did go to Nineveh, and some see this going as obedience. However, chapter IV makes clear that he went in the vain hope that he could bend God's will to his own. His rebellion masqueraded as obedience.

Now Nineveh was: For a discussion of this phrase, see Appendix I, p. 124.

Three days journey in breadth: For a discussion of the size of Nineveh, see Appendix I, p. 124.

3:4. *A day's journey:* This phrase seems to indicate that Jonah was one-third of the way through the city, and hence near the center, before he began to preach. However, it can also be interpreted to mean that Jonah began preaching as soon as he arrived and that he had gone through one-third of the city when the people responded overwhelmingly. In either case the response was phenomenal.

Forty days: The Septuagint says "three days." Some have suggested that three days fits better into the rapid movement of the story. It would mean that when Jonah went out on the hillside to watch he expected the destruction immediately, since it had taken him three days to walk through the city. The question would then arise as to why he built a booth to sit in. Also it is possible that the Septuagint reading "three days" in 3:4 is a slip of the copyist's pen, being unconsciously confused with the "three days" in 3:3. Actually the point to the story is the same whether it is three days or forty days.

3:5. *People of Nineveh:* What language did Jonah use to communicate with them? The author does not say. However, it is possible that the Syrian language, Aramaic, was a kind of *lingua franca* in the area, as *Isaiah* 36:11 seems to indicate.

Believed: The Hebrew construction used here is the same as that used in *Genesis* 15:6 where it signifies Abraham's trust. The Ninevites not only believed that God would carry out his threat. They went further and trusted in God, a mark of genuine repentance.

God: It is interesting to note that the word *Elohim* (God) and not *Yahweh* is used here. Perhaps the author is suggesting that the people believed God and not the narrow tribal god that Jonah wanted Yahweh to be.

Put on sackcloth: A sign of complete self-abasement. (See *Joel* 1:8, 13-14; *Jeremiah* 6:26; *Ezekiel* 27:30-31; and *Job* 2:8.) The fact that the king removes his royal robes, puts on sackcloth, and joins the people sitting in ashes indicates the thoroughness of Nineveh's repentance. The instant readiness with which the Ninevites responded to God's word is in stark contrast to the slowness and obstinacy of Israel.

3:6. *King of Nineveh:* See Appendix I, pp. 124-125.

3:7. *Man nor beast:* The inclusion of animals in a fast was not an uncommon practice among both the Persians and the Jews. Its purpose was to make the fast more thorough and thus to impress upon deity the great sincerity of the repentance. Of course the animals would not literally put on sackcloth and they could not call mightily unto God, but the picture of genuine repentance for the whole city is clear.

3:9. *God may yet repent:* Note the parallel in *Joel* 2:14 and *Exodus* 32:12. The hope expressed by the king finds a solid basis in God's declared policy toward nations. *Jeremiah*

18:7-8 asserts: "If at any time I declare concerning a nation or a kingdom, that I will pluck up and break down and destroy it, and if that nation, concerning which I have spoken turns from its evil, I will repent of the evil that I intended to do to it." Also see exegesis of "God Repented" in next chapter.

Footnotes

[1] This is the title of a famous sermon preached by Thomas Chalmers. See *Protestant Pulpit*, ed. Andrew W. Blackwood (New York: Abingdon-Cokesbury, 1947), pp. 50-62. Reprinted from *The Works of Thomas Chalmers* (New York: Robert Carter and Bros., 1830), Vol. II.

[2] See George M. Landes, "The 'Three Days and Three Nights' Motif in Jonah 2:1," *Journal of Biblical Literature*, December 1967, pp. 446-450.

[3] E. B. Pusey, *The Minor Prophets* (New York: Funk and Wagnalls, 1885), pp. 384-387.

[4] Landes, *op. cit.*

[5] See "The Kerygma of the Book of Jonah," *Interpretation*, January 1967, pp. 4-31.

V
MISSION

"Better For Me To Die": Obstinacy

*When God saw what they did, how they turned from their
evil way, God repented of the evil which he said he
would do to them; and he did not do it. But it displeased
Jonah exceedingly, and he was angry. And he prayed to the
Lord and said, "I pray thee, Lord, is not this what I said
when I was yet in my country? That is why I made haste to
flee to Tarshish; for I knew that thou art a gracious God and
merciful, slow to anger, and abounding in steadfast love,
and repentest of evil. Therefore, now, O Lord, take my life
from me, I beseech thee, for it is better for me to die than
to live." And the Lord said, "Do you do well to be angry?"*
—Jonah 3:10-4:4

Jonah's sermon to the Ninevites was possibly the shortest
ever preached. It contained only eight words: "Yet forty days
and Nineveh shall be overthrown." But it was also the most
effective ever preached. In the last chapter we looked at the
amazing results it produced. Imagine! A whole city converted
with eight words! What preacher would not be happy! But
not Jonah. In fact, instead of being overjoyed, he was exceedingly angry (4:1).

Here the story reaches its crucial point. Verse 4:2 is the
fulcrum around which the entire message revolves. Jonah declares that he had known all along that God is "gracious and
merciful, slow to anger; and abounding in steadfast love, and
repentest of evil." This verse with slight variation is a quotation
of *Exodus* 34:6. The reference is made for the specific purpose
of emphasizing that the covenant applies to all—even the
hated Ninevites. Actually Jonah (Israel) had known this all

75

along, and it was precisely this application of the covenant to all peoples that he (Israel) was rebelling against.

How human the story is. Jonah is trapped. He can no longer argue, so he gets mad. His name may mean "dove," but he is far from gentle. Realizing that it is now impossible to escape the full implication of God's universal love and mercy, he goes into a rage. He begins scolding God. If we translate the polite biblical language into popular jargon, Jonah is saying (4:2), "I told you so! I knew you wouldn't go through with it. I knew you'd soften and chicken out! That's why I went to Tarshish in the first place. I didn't want to be embarrassed. Make a pronouncement and then have you back down on me! I knew you were a Nineveh-loving God. I'd rather be dead!"

Why was Jonah so angry with God for showing mercy to the Ninevites? On the surface it does not make sense. How could anyone be angry with God for sparing repentant sinners and particularly the little children? The enigma becomes clear, however, if we stop and think for a moment. In sparing Nineveh, God had done three things. First, he had wounded Jonah's pride. A prophet's reputation depended on the fulfillment of his predictions. Deuteronomy 18:22 says, "When a prophet speaks . . . if the word does not come to pass . . . that is a word which the Lord has not spoken; the prophet has spoken it presumptuously." Jonah had failed and now he would be an object of ridicule. It is an ugly picture, but the author in no wise pulls his punches. Here is a pitiful little prophet nursing his wounded pride and demanding that God vindicate him by destroying the Ninevites.

Second, in sparing Nineveh God had declared that Jonah must forgive the Ninevites for all their atrocities and, as noted above, these atrocities had been horrible. Jonah refused to do it. The writer of Jonah thus contends that Jonah (Israel), in refusing to forgive and to be merciful, was actually rejecting the God of Abraham, Isaac and Jacob—the God of the covenant. Israel, he says, is not willing for God to be merciful and insists that the steadfast love and mercy expressed in Exodus 34:6 must have a "For Jews Only" sign upon it.

Third, in sparing Nineveh God made clear that Ninevites and Israelites are equal in his sight. If the people of Nineveh are the object of God's special love and mercy, then God's concern for Ninevites must be as great as his concern for

Israelites. And if this is true, then are not the two on an equal footing? What, then, becomes of the Israelites' favored position? Hebrew superiority is struck a fatal blow. The Ninevites can no longer be looked down upon as inferior—as the "lesser breeds without the law." They must be accepted as God's children, too.

Jonah could not take it. Such a demand made him furious. His feelings were so deeply ingrained that he simply could not accept God's demand. We need to be sympathetic with Jonah at this point. God's demand cut across the grain of everything that he had been taught and ran counter to the deepest feelings of his nature. Surely we can understand how Jonah felt. To accept equality with the Gentiles was emotionally impossible for him. It destroyed the foundation on which his entire life had been built. Accepting ethnic or racial groups in our own community as equals may also cut across the grain of everything we have been taught and run counter to our deepest feelings. It may undermine the foundation on which our lives have been built.

"These Ninevites as good as Jews? Associate with them as equals? Never! I'd rather die first! Why this would mean the complete destruction of our kosher laws and our distinctiveness! Our restrictions against eating with foreigners would have to go. They might even expect to be served in our restaurants. Impossible! It would mean the end of our cherished way of life." With a tenacity almost unbelievable, the Hebrew people steadfastly refused to accept other peoples as equals. So deeply ingrained was this attitude that for many it became simply a constituent part of what it meant to be a Jew. The bitterness growing out of the exile and the years subsequent to it seemed to increase rather than decrease. Even in Jesus' day the attitude continued. Peter, you will recall, in talking to Cornelius and his household, reminded them: "I need not tell you that a Jew is forbidden by his religion to visit or associate with a man of another race." (Acts 10:28, New English Bible).

Turning to Galatians we discover that eating with Gentiles was an issue not only among the Jews, but also in the early church. Paul records that even Peter, prince of the apostles, "drew back [from eating with the Gentiles] and separated himself." Paul says, "I opposed him to his face, because he stood condemned" (Galatians 2:11-12). Or go to Luke 4:16-30.

This is the account of Jesus' sermon in Nazareth. At first the people all "spoke well of him" (verse 22). Then suddenly they turned against him, drove him out of the city and almost killed him. Why? Read verses 25-27, and you will see:

But in truth, I tell you, there were many widows in Israel in the days of Elijah, when the heaven was shut up three years and six months, when there came a great famine over all the land; and Elijah was sent to none of them but only to Zarephath, in the land of Sidon, to a woman who was a widow. And there were many lepers in Israel in the time of the prophet Elisha; and none of them was cleansed, but only Naaman the Syrian.

Verse 28 continues: "When they heard this, all in the synagogue were filled with wrath." In other words, Jesus was declaring that a Sidonese widow and a Syrian leper were favored above all the Hebrews of that time. Note the three classes mentioned: Gentile, leper, woman. The pious Jew of Jesus' day thanked God daily that he was not a Gentile, a leper or a woman. These classes were at the bottom rung of society. Yet Jesus had the audacity to point out that God favored them above all the Jews. This was heresy of the worst kind. These were truly fighting words. The people reacted violently, as had Jonah four hundred years before. Jonah in effect, was saying:

"Accept the Gentiles as equals? Why how could we possibly do that? They might want to move into our neighborhoods. And what would it do to the temple? Have the Gentiles in the inner court? How utterly absurd can one be? And what would happen to our schools if the Gentiles were admitted? No, Lord, I could never accept that. I'd rather die first. 'Therefore now, O Lord, take my life from me, I beseech thee, for it is better for me to die than to live.' If this is the kind of world you are running, count me out. Why, I'd rather be dead than to have to live in community with those Ninevites!"

Rather die than live! What a modern ring this has. It seems to gather up in one tortured phrase the anguished dilemma of our world. Since the dawn of history, we have rebelled against both our creaturehood and our humanhood. Our first sin was to deny our creaturehood—to try to have the knowledge of

God—to be like God (*Genesis* 3:5), rather than being creatures in the image of God (*Genesis* 1:27). Our second sin was to deny our humanhood, our relationship to others of God's children—"And Cain rose up against his brother Abel and killed him" (Genesis 4:8). Theologians speak of this universal experience of humanity as the Fall. Then they go on to talk about our fallenness and our sinfulness. But whatever we call it, the fact remains that without the redeeming power of Christ in our lives, we choose to be damned rather than to obey God, to die rather than to live in community with all of God's people.

We see this drama of the human race in bold relief in the story of Jonah. If any Old Testament character ever rebelled against both creaturehood and humanhood, it was Jonah. He tried to be like God. He sat in judgment on Nineveh. He even sat in judgment on God. He tried to order God around. He tried to outsmart God by maneuvering God into a position in which he would be forced to destroy Nineveh. Jonah's terse, categorical, "Yet forty days and Nineveh shall be overthrown" was deliberate. It held out no hope.[1] As a prophetic declaration —the word of the Lord—its fulfillment was mandatory (Isaiah 55:11). Jonah was thus saying to God: "Now you must either put up or shut up. You must either destroy Nineveh or prove yourself a liar!" Jonah knew that God was softhearted (4:2) and would need to be prodded into doing his painful duty. Jonah was perfectly sure that he knew better than God how to run the world. The matter was quite simple: Destroy all your enemies. God's children? How absurd! They were nothing but Ninevites! Away with them!

Clearly Jonah's hatred was excessive. His vindictiveness went beyond all reason. But before we criticize him let us look at ourselves. Does not Jonah's vindictive spirit point to one of the deepest problems of our twentieth century? Our present world seems determined on a scale more vast than Jonah ever dreamed, to die rather than live in community with all peoples. Witness the tensions, the strife, the widespread hatred, the callous indifference, the flagrant injustice, the brutal repressions, the bloody wars, the violence, the senseless fratricide. And what so often escapes us in all of this is that fratricide is also deicide, for did not Christ say, "As you did it to one of the least of these my brethren, you did it to me"? (Matthew 25:40). In killing others we kill God.

Consider the many subtle ways of killing. We do not have to use a knife or a gun. By denying human dignity and basic human rights we have killed the highest and fullest potentiality in millions because of some artificial distinction such as race or sex or religious and ethnic background or economic status in life. We have usually thought of Matthew 25:40 in terms of gaining merit, of doing good to Christ by doing good—a cup of cold water, a visit in prison—to one of the "least of these." But does not the verse also mean that the hurts we inflict on others are also inflicted on Christ?

Obviously all of us inflict hurts on others unintentionally due to human weakness, and God is merciful and forgiving when we are humble and repentant. But is it different when we intentionally maintain systems that inflict suffering on others by denying them human dignity? Such systems—cruelty systems— have been sanctioned by our laws and maintained by force and violence. They have consigned some of the least of these (and incidentally some of the greatest of these also) to an inferior place and have cowed and browbeaten them into accepting this inferiority—into "staying in their place." Millions of personalities have been warped, twisted, prevented full growth and thus hurt irreparably. In a very real sense they have been killed. Is it possible that we have done this to Christ? I am sure that most of us have never thought of it this way, and such a thought may be quite disturbing, but is there any other way to interpret Matthew 25:40? Possibly our problem is that we have never really put ourselves in the other's place in order to feel what he feels. Surely this was Jonah's problem.

Rather die than live! From seething Africa to explosive Ireland; from tortured Asia to turbulent America tensions mount and in many subtle ways our selfishness leads us to choose death in myriad forms rather than truly live as God calls us to live in Christ. Constant eruptions of racial strife; class conflicts; riots that respect neither lives nor property; terrorists striking innocent people; reprisals that kill women and children; standing feuds that totter ever on the edge of erup- tion; neighbors who will not speak; wars where brother is pitted against brother and computers rain senseless death on innocent people; vicious economic struggles where people count for nothing; hatred striking in dark streets and alleys; bombs blasting businesses, churches, homes and airplanes; shotguns on lonely highways—the list is endless.

Rather die than live! This is indeed the tragedy of our twentieth century. Jonah still walks our streets, boards our ships and sits under our gourd vines.

Study Questions

1. This chapter speaks about the vicious cycle of hate and revenge. How can the cycle be broken?

2. Why are issues of race so explosive?

3. What is the root of prejudice? Some educators say that actions produce attitudes and not vice versa. Is this true? If it is, what actions could we initiate in our community that might change attitudes and reduce prejudice?

4. What are some ways in which we might move beyond our present stage of nationalism and racism to world peace and harmony?

5. Has there been a lessening or an increase in prejudice in your community in the past three years? Why? Could a study of the causes of increase or decrease in prejudice help us to take positive steps to eliminate it?

6. Why did God's forgiveness of the Ninevites make Jonah so angry?

"Jonah . . . Made a Booth For Himself": Complacency

Then Jonah went out of the city and sat to the east of the city, and made a booth for himself there. He sat under it in the shade, till he should see what would become of the city.　　　　　　　　　—Jonah 4:5

Whatever else we may say about Jonah, one thing is certain, he had determination. He did not give up easily. Maybe he thought his temper tantrum would cause God to reconsider. Or maybe he did not believe God would really spare the city. The people of Nineveh were wicked—no question about that. Jonah was one of those hardhearted moralists who are long on judgment and short on mercy. He was the kind who would throw the "sinners" out of the church. He went out on the hillside, because he wanted the pleasure of witnessing Nineveh's

destruction, if it did happen. Looking in the direction of Jerusalem (something every pious Jew cherished) and anticipating
the destruction of Nineveh could afford Jonah two exquisite
pleasures at once.

With this development, the story nears its climax. God is
making ever clearer the heart of Israel's rebellion. Here we see
in bold relief the self-satisfied Hebrew at ease in Zion, watch-
ing eagerly for the destruction of his enemies. The heat on the
barren hillside is intense. So Jonah builds a booth where he
can sit in comfort while Nineveh burns. A vine grows up to
shade the booth and make it more comfortable. How God
provides for his own! Then tragedy strikes. The vine dies.
Jonah, exposed to the heat of the sun, is furious. How can God
possibly allow his "chosen" to suffer so?

This picture of the comfortable Hebrew at ease under a
gourd vine strikes at the heart of our own rebellion and points
to one of the crucial problems of our age: the appalling
complacency of an affluent society in the face of widespread
human suffering and mass poverty. Jesus pointed to the same
problem in his parable of the rich farmer (Luke 12:16-21).
This man, like Jonah, thought of himself as God's favorite.
He thought that great blessings had come to him because of
who he was. Read the story again, and note the number of
times the first personal pronoun is used. Almost every other
word is "I," "my" or "mine."

Is this a picture of our society? Do we, like the rich fool,
repeat over and over again, "I, my, mine"—and hoard our
crops in bigger and bigger barns? Storage is of course essential in our complex economic world. But to spend millions
of dollars to store surplus food (full production could produce
even greater surpluses) while millions of people are hungry,
surely indicates a serious problem. In the early 1960's we
were spending close to two million dollars a day to store our
surplus food. In 1972 the figure was still approximately three-
fourths of a million.[2] Most assuredly we could not simply give
our surpluses away, even if we wanted to, without disrupting
the economy of other countries, as well as our own. Even if
our surplus food were given away, it would be eaten in a few
weeks and the problem would still be with us. Doles are not
the answer. World economic structures are vast and complicated, and there are no easy solutions.

But the fact remains: we build larger and larger barns while half the world starves. America with six percent of the world's population consumes roughly 50 percent of the world's non-renewable resources utilized each year.[3] We throw away in our garbage cans each day enough to feed the hungry millions of India. Some way must be found for a more equitable distribution of that which God has placed here for all peoples. Does it make sense for an overstuffed society to spend millions of dollars on reducing diets while half the world has no diet at all? Surely some way could be found to remove this fundamental inconsistency if we really cared enough. Has our affluence led us to accept with complaceny a world that has both a storage problem and a starvation problem? Can we be content to spend millions of dollars for storage while millions of people starve?

The principle stated here applies not only to the affluent west, but to all "rich farmers" everywhere who are storing and stuffing while people starve. The wealthy few are not confined to one geographical area. About five years ago while we were living in the Philippines, a wealthy landowner and industrialist gave a thirty-fifth wedding anniversary party at his palatial home. On the grounds he strung up forty thousand light bulbs. He erected a huge fountain in his garden which spewed champagne instead of water. He chartered planes and flew fifteen hundred guests in from all over the world. A special band from the United States reportedly cost $100,000. He is reported in the newspapers to have spent close to a half million dollars on the party. As I drove by his palatial home every day on my way to the Union Theological Seminary and looked at the hovels put together with scraps of wood, tin and cardboard just outside his lovely gardens, I could not help thinking of the feudalism of Czarist Russia in 1919 when the communist revolution broke out. People in these hovels in Manila were existing on a per capita income of twenty cents a day. As I watched the angry demonstrations against the industrialist's useless display of opulence, I wrote: "How long can this kind of thing go on without a bloody revolution?" It took no prophet to foresee the kind of turmoil that has brought Philippine society today to the brink of catastrophe and that has put the entire country under martial law. The trouble has just begun. It is going to become much worse unless some basic problems are dealt with quickly.

It is quite true that there is a growing concern today for the poor in all nations and especially for the mass poverty in underdeveloped nations. Demands for a more equitable distribution of the world's resources are being heard and much is being done. For this we can be grateful. But the fact remains that the concern has not yet reached the stage of producing truly significant action. In spite of all that is being done, the gap between the rich and the poor widens.[4] We have not begun to deal with the problem as though we meant to solve it.

In 1965 the per capita annual income in the 33 poorest countries of the world with an aggregate population of 1,691,000,000 (roughly half the world's population) was $69, or approximately 19¢ a day.[5] By 1971 some of these nations had made small gains but others had either declined or remained static, showing small ups and downs from year to year. India, for example, the second largest nation in the world, with almost one fifth of the world's population, declined in per capita income from $88 in 1965 to $70 in 1967 and rose back to $80 by 1971. The fifth largest nation, Indonesia, declined from $85 in 1965 to $65 in 1971. **Nigeria, the** largest nation in Africa in population, declined from $78 in 1965 to $70 in 1971.[6]

In contrast to this static condition in the highly populous underdeveloped areas, the per capita income has been soaring in the United States and elsewhere in the industrial west. Looking at the period we have just been talking about, we discover that from 1963 to 1967 the U.S. per capita income increased from $2532 to $3266, or by a total of $734.[7] The *increase only* in U.S. income in four years was 10 times the *total per capita* income in India. U.S. per capita income already 30 times that of India increased in four years to 40 times. By 1971 U.S. per capita income had risen to $4135,[8] which is 50 times that of India. Each year the total U.S. annual income, already over a trillion dollars, increases by 60 billion. This increase alone is equal to the total annual income of all of South America.[9]

The contrast in our "Lopsided World" [10] is even more stark when we realize that per capita income figures do not tell the full story since they are national averages and include the rich as well as the poor. In the Philippines, for example, where the writer is most familiar having lived there for 16 years, the per capita income in 1971 was 37 cents a day.[11] But the wide disparity between the rich and the poor left many millions existing on 25 cents a day or less. Great masses—probably two-thirds of the world's people—exist on less than the average American spends each day for cokes, candy and chewing gum. It is no wonder that half of the world's people suffer from serious malnutrition.[12] The damage is both physical and mental because the brain of an undernourished child cannot develop normally. Often people in poverty areas are accused of being lazy, lacking in ambition and ability. The fact is that they are victims of the poverty cycle, their bodies and minds not having had the nourishment necessary for normal development. The crucial question is how to break out of this vicious cycle.

The basic problem is the problem of power. In the words of Paul, we wrestle "against the principalities, against the powers, against the world rulers of this present darkness." In our vastly interdependent world, power structures—economic, technological, political, military and many other kinds—have emerged that determine the welfare and the destiny of millions. These power structures are controlled by wealth and become extremely impersonal. Often without any evil intent or malevolent design, they, nevertheless, because of the natural economic principle of wealth producing wealth, favor the haves over the have-nots. The truth of this claim is amply borne out by the fact that with all of the sincere efforts over the past twenty years to develop the underdeveloped nations, the already developed nations have developed several times faster than the underdeveloped nations. Of course there are many factors within the underdeveloped nations that impede development. But there is also the fact of power structures either wittingly or unwittingly taking advantage of the powerless.

For example, shipping companies pay stevedores in Los Angeles five dollars an hour to load a ship. When the same cargo is unloaded in Manila these same shipowners pay the stevedores one dollar a day. The stevedore in Los Angeles receives forty times the wage of the stevedore in Manila. Why? The stevedore in Los Angeles has power, the power of U.S. economy, labor unions and the threat of strike. The stevedore in

Manila is completely powerless; he has to take what he can get; so our world economy takes advantage of him. Or note that from 1950 to 1964 private companies in America invested $10 billion in South America. But they took out of Latin America in profits $21 billion.[13]

Uncomfortable though it may be, we must face the fact that today millions of people are locked into tragic economic structures that perpetuate poverty. Unless these structures are drastically changed, the people trapped in them will remain powerless to break out of the poverty cycle. This is why mass poverty not only persists but grows at an alarming rate in our world. What the masses are clamoring for is not doles but economic development, not handouts but simple justice. In a world of international economic anarchy, however, it is impossible for the kinds of structures that have brought about more economic justice in the U.S.A. ever to emerge. Antitrust laws, fair labor practices, fair interest rates, protection for farmers in the form of crop loans and price supports, protection for the small businessman, protection against all kinds of unfair competition or exploitation on a world scale presuppose the kind of world government that does not exist today.

What is demanded on the economic front as well as all others is a new, bold strategy—a crash program for development on a worldwide scale.[14] This will demand professional and technical expertise, as well as careful planning and more careful execution of plans. But more than all this, it will demand a deep spiritual conversion on the part of the wealthy haves, the favored few. The haves seem to be perfectly happy with development as long as it brings profit and a rising standard of living for themselves, but to forego profits and to undergo sacrifice is another matter. Evidence seems to mount that the haves are not willing to do this. Every time any move is made to give a break to some underdeveloped area of the world, pressure groups in North America and Western Europe, sensing a possible disadvantage to themselves, enter strong protests and lobby to defeat it. Some excuse our lethargy and complacency by saying, "Social change is slow. It takes time." Such a statement may be convincing to the haves, but not to the one whose family is starving. The demand for revolution today arises from the fact that slow change is not working. Are we to doom another generation of a billion people to dwarfed and crippled lives with the suave, complacent explanation, "It takes time?" The swelling cry of today is now, not tomorrow.

The frustrating question for us is: what specifically can be done and how? It is sobering to realize that even our missionary endeavors designed to help the poor and oppressed are caught up in the same dilemma. Most of the Christian missionaries in the world are a part of, and thus representative of, the affluent few. Many missionaries feel guilty and are greatly disturbed by this fact, but until now no one has come up with a satisfactory answer. In a recent meeting of around two hundred missionaries, an effort was made to formulate a statement as a basis for action concerning the developing nations. After much discussion the statement was ready, but at the crucial moment of its adoption one young missionary arose and proposed that the following words be placed at the end: "We recognize, however, the utter hypocrisy of this statement because we know quite well that even as we vote for it, we missionaries will continue to be over-fed, over-clothed and over-housed as members of the affluent society." The young missionary's proposal brought everyone up sharp. What can we do? What are we willing to do?

Yet, a startling fact confronts us today. For the first time in history there is the real possibility of an abundance for all. Modern technology in both production and distribution makes it actually possible to abolish poverty from the face of the earth. The only question is: Do we care enough to make this possibility a reality? This is the question posed by the book of *Jonah*. Do we really care? Or are we content to build a booth around the status quo in a world where we are favorites? "And Jonah . . . made a booth for himself."

Study Questions

1. In a world where technology both in production and distribution makes possible the abolition of poverty, what can we do to see that the possibility speedily becomes an actuality?

2. Realizing that the U.S. with six percent of the world's population consumes roughly 50 percent of the world's non-renewable resources and that it enjoys an affluence beyond even the wildest dreams of two-thirds (roughly two billion) of the world's people who live on a per capita income of 20 to 30 cents a day, are we willing to sacrifice even a little of this

affluence in order that others may at least have a healthy diet and decent standard of living?

3. Should U.S. economic policies regarding world trade and foreign investments be changed where they affect adversely the developing nations? Should the churches lobby in congress for such changes? Should this become a number one issue in American politics? Should we seek to influence the boards of directors of large corporations? If so, how?

"You Pity the Plant": Callousness

And the LORD God appointed a plant, and made it come up over Jonah, that it might be a shade over his head to save him from his discomfort. So Jonah was exceedingly glad because of the plant. But when dawn came up the next day, God appointed a worm which attacked the plant, so that it withered. When the sun rose, God appointed a sultry east wind, and the sun beat upon the head of Jonah so that he was faint, and he asked that he might die, and said, "It is better for me to die than to live."

But God said to Jonah, "Do you do well to be angry for the plant?" And he said, "I do well to be angry, angry enough to die." And the LORD said, "You pity the plant, for which you did no labor, nor did you make it grow, which came into being in a night, and perished in a night. And should I not pity Nineveh, that great city, in which there are more than a hundred and twenty thousand persons who do not know their right hand from their left, and also much cattle?

—Jonah 4:6-11

In one last desperate effort to get through to Jonah, God raises up a plant and then mercilessly destroys it. It is an object lesson, but the lesson falls on deaf ears (see Exegesis). Jonah is adamant and immovable. It should be carefully noted that, though Jonah is left speechless at the end of the book, there is not the slightest hint that God has convinced him or that he has changed his mind. The author is too realistic to suggest that prejudice yields to reason so easily. Look for a moment in retrospect at the picture the author has painted. First, it is the heathen sailors whose compassion places in bold relief the vindictiveness of Jonah. Now it is God's love which stands over against Jonah's hate. God is deeply concerned about his people. Jonah is deeply concerned about his plant.

"Plants" or people? This is a burning issue in the twentieth century. There is no doubt that we have been putting "plants" above people. Christians put plants above people when they joined in the exploitation of China a century ago. The British went to war to force opium (a plant!) on the Chinese, defeated them, made them pay for the beating and then forced them to accept the opium and to grant special concessions to Britishers in China. The most significant part of this episode, from our point of view, is that the church came in for a healthy share of the benefits. Asians were not slow to observe this readiness of the church to accept the fruits of colonial exploitation.

K. M. Panikkar comments, "It is also significant that out of the unconscionable indemnities exacted from China, the churches received a considerable portion. The missions thus started by benefiting from the humiliations of China and by being identified in the eyes of the Chinese with aggressions against their country." For this reason, he says, the treaty clauses "wrote the ultimate doom of Christian activity in China. To have believed that a religion which grew up under the protection of foreign powers, especially under humiliating conditions following defeat, would be tolerated when the nation recovered its authority shows extreme short-sightedness." [15] And still Christians blame the failure of the church in China on the Ninevites (Communists).

Christians likewise put plants above people in the Congo. Pierre Rijikman, governor-general of the Congo for many years, described the Belgian policy as *Dominer pour servir*—"Dominate in order to serve." However, George W. Carpenter points out that "big business, the Roman Catholic missions, and the colonial government formed a triumvirate," which saw to it that the major service was to Belgium.[16] This dominate-in-order-to-serve policy, for instance, meant that in over two hundred years of Belgian rule, not a single university or college was established in the Congo. The first one was opened in the 1950's. It graduated its first class of sixteen students in 1959. Only a handful of Congolese were ever permitted to study overseas. Therefore, in 1960 when independence came to the Congo, it is reported that there were less than a dozen college graduates in a total Congolese population of fourteen million.[17]

Europeans in general went to Africa to seek their fortune. They reveled in its rich natural resources. They mined its gold. They developed its power. They cultivated its soil. They promoted its trade. They were greatly excited over its plants. But for its people they had little concern—except as the "natives" could be used to serve their own purposes. As someone has aptly said, our chief concern has been the welfare of wealth, not the welfare of people. This intolerable condition unfortunately still continues today on all six continents.

Of course no one would suggest that the issues involved are simple. Europeans and other Westerners have done much good in Africa and Asia, and credit should be given where credit is due. Moreover, the task of changing the prevailing conditions is staggering. Vast interacting political, economic and social systems render human relationships unbelievably intricate. There are no easy answers. Improved medical services that cut the infant mortality rate may only increase the number of people on the starvation list. Economic aid may make the rich richer, the poor poorer, and only serve to entrench an oppressive regime because needed reforms are not made. On the other hand, reforms too hastily implemented can create more problems than they solve.

But with all the complexity of a technological age, the basic human dilemma on a worldwide scale still confronts us: "Plants" or People? And the fact also remains that we could do something—we could find solutions—if enough of us really wanted to. We cannot blame circumstances, or conditions, or technological complexities, or the communists, or the colonialists, or the establishment, or the "bad people," or anything else. We must simply admit that we are Jonahs. God still says to us, "You pity the plant."

Study Questions

1. Are there ways in which we put "plants" above people in our cities and communities? in our churches? in our homes? our personal lives? How?

2. None of us would consciously put plants above people; yet we know it has happened and is happening. Suggest ways in which we might structure our society to prevent this.

3. What is the meaning of "the whole gospel for the whole man for the whole world"?

"And Also Much Cattle": Love

The words, ". . . and also much cattle," bring the book of *Jonah* to a masterful close. God is concerned even with the animals. Recall that they too had been included in the king's decree: "Let neither man nor beast, herd nor flock taste anything" (3:7). And now in the closing verse God does not forget them. Is this not beautiful? The picture of God's all-embracing love has reached the most complete expression to be found anywhere in the Old Testament. Only one brush stroke is yet needed, and that stroke must be penned on a cross. He, who later revealed the Father fully, put it this way: "Are not five sparrows sold for two pennies? And not one of them is forgotten before God" (*Luke* 12:6). The reference to the cattle also highlights the insignificance of a plant when compared with animals, much less with people. To pity a plant and despise people—or even animals—is the ultimate rejection of the God of Abraham, Isaac and Jacob, the God of Amos, Hosea, Isaiah and Jeremiah.

The abrupt ending of the book leaves a picture forever etched in the memory: Jonah pouting over his pitifully puny plant, while the great heart of God reaches out to his lost children. The Ninevites are saved, not because they are good, but precisely because they are unworthy and have recognized it. This is a *sola fide*—salvation by faith alone. Jonah is lost —left sitting out on a barren hillside—because he knows he is good and, therefore, neither needs to forgive nor to repent and be forgiven. It is true that God has the last word and that Jonah is silenced. Also the traditional interpretation usually assumes that Jonah was at last converted, but this inference is not warranted by anything in the text. As already noted, there is no hint of even a slight change in Jonah's attitude. Rather, it seems that his pride, his self-centeredness, his burning hatred, and his unforgiving spirit doom him to a self-created hell.

Throughout this study we have called attention to the many ways in which Jonah is our contemporary. There is no character in the Bible who epitomizes humankind quite like Jonah. The absurdity of Jonah's attitude toward Nineveh is clear to us, while the utterly startling way in which we are so much like him eludes us. There could be no clearer confirmation of the theological doctrine of original sin: we are unable to see that we are unable to see. We must have "prevenient grace." God must open our eyes. But this prevenient grace can only come when we are willing to surrender and become like little children: open, humble, receptive. Jonah is the epitome of all that rejects this childlike faith. We therefore leave him a forlorn, dejected figure on a barren hillside, a pitiful package all wrapped up in himself.

The question is now squarely before us: Will we surrender our own lives and our loves to God? Or will we remain stubborn Jonahs clinging desperately to our own little hells? Will we choose to live or to die? Though surely the hour is late, there is yet time to turn from our self-preoccupation and stubbornness, walk down off the hillside into the midst of God's Nineveh and surrender ourselves to God's loving purpose for the world. From the main street of Nineveh there could yet come in our day the word of God that liberates and sets us free to live.

The book of *Jonah* marks an epoch. The day Nineveh was spared, humanity's understanding of God took a giant leap forward. No doubt Jonah felt forsaken as he sat alone on the hillside. From his point of view God had let him down. He must have experienced what has been called in recent years the "absence of God" or the "death of God." In fact it would seem that a god did die that day: the narrow, nationalistic, ruthless, racial deity Jonah worshipped. Tragically, however, this god has not remained dead. He has been resurrected and still continues to stalk the earth commanding the allegiance of millions.

The vision of the prophet who wrote the book of *Jonah* was so grand that the people of his day could not grasp it—or if they did, they rejected it as too idealistic. The dream was so audacious that even after more than two thousand years we seem not much closer to it. But with all the convulsions of our twentieth century, we may be nearer than we think. This may be the darkness before the dawn. At least it can be, if we will hear *Jonah* speak. In the words of William Scarlett:

> One cannot read it [*Jonah*] without experiencing some of the glowing contagion of the author's dream. And he cannot put it down without wistfully saying to himself, "If men only would, if men only could, 'Earth [might] be fair, and all her people one.' " [18]

1. Describe an imaginary scene on the hillside and write in your own words the conversation that may have taken place between God and Jonah. Some have suggested that God gave Jonah a sharp, stern scolding. Others have suggested a tender but firm, "Jonah! These are my children!" Still others have imagined a long argument or conversation. Write your own. One suggestion is found on pages 119-120.

Exegesis

3:10. *God repented*. The word *repent* does not imply that God has sinned. It is used in the sense of "change one's mind." Parallels may be observed in *Exodus* 32:14, *II Samuel* 24:16 and *Amos* 7:3, 6. The Bible does not hesitate to assert that when a person turns from sin (repents), God must adopt a different course of action in order to be consistent with his own nature. It is not that God's intention is changed, but rather that a person's repentance opens new possibilities for God, possibilities that are inherent in human freedom. Nineveh's repentance brings God's forgiveness because God's very nature is to be "merciful, slow to anger, and abounding in steadfast love" (4:2).

4:1. *He was angry*. This verse makes clear that Jonah did not go to Nineveh to save the people. The irony of Jonah's anger is that he is not only mad at God but also mad at himself. He now realizes that in yielding to God's demand that he go to Nineveh, he has, against his will, become the instrument of the people's salvation. He reasons that without his warning, the city would have been destroyed. This thought is so bitter that he wants to die. The proclamation which he thought would trap God and force the destruction of Nlneveh has backfired. It has brought about the salvation of the city.

4:2. *And he prayed*: Jonah's prayer is not a prayer at all, but a denunciation of God. He has the audacity to stand up and to chastise God for what God has done.

Thou art a gracious God: Jonah's words reflect, and in part are quoted directly from, the ancient covenant between Israel and God as found in *Exodus* 34:6-7. *Joel* 2:13 quotes the same verse with a slight variation. Jonah's version is closer to that of Joel and may have been taken from him. The author of *Jonah* uses these words from *Exodus* for the specific purpose of drawing a sharp contrast between Jonah's attitude (the common attitude of most Jews in the post-exilic period) and the attitude of Yahweh in the original covenant with Israel. Jonah (Israel) is in rebellion not only against Yahweh, but also against the covenant which expresses the true Israelite heritage. There is a note of both impatience and sarcasm in Jonah's voice, which heightens the contrast. Also it is significant that Jonah, not God, quotes the passage. Jonah actually knew all along what God's true nature is.

4:3. *Take my life from me:* An echo of I Kings 19:4 where Elijah says the same thing. But Elijah's reasons were exactly the opposite of Jonah's. Elijah wanted to die because he felt that everyone but he had forsaken Yahweh. Jonah wanted to die because several hundred thousand people had turned to Yahweh.

4:4. *Jonah, do you do well to be angry?* God's reply to Jonah's prayer is a calm, poised and gentle but searching question, a superb way for a father to answer the temper tantrum of a sulking child.

4:5. *East of the city:* The side opposite Palestine. Jonah had passed through the entire city. Looking down on Nineveh from this vantage point he would also be looking in the direction of Jerusalem.

Booth: Some kind of temporary shade, probably made of branches and covered with leaves or grass.

Till he should see: Even after God had made plain his intention to spare Nineveh Jonah still clung to the hope that the city might be destroyed. A more stubborn, vindictive character one cannot find in all the pages of world literature.

4:6. *LORD God:* The phrase is probably used here by the author to indicate that the LORD (Yahweh) is not the tribal god Jonah wishes him to be but is identical with the God (Elohim) on whom the king calls (3:9), a universal God whose love includes all people.

Appointed: Note the stress on God's action in the book of *Jonah*: God commanded Jonah to go to Nineveh; God sent the storm; God provided the fish; God commanded the fish to vomit out Jonah; God caused the plant to grow; God sent the worm to attack it; God sent the east wind to blow on Jonah; God rebukes Jonah; God has the last word.

Plant: Probably a castor-oil plant (*recinus communis*), noted for its rapid growth. The King James Version translates it *gourd,* and it is possible that it was the bottle-gourd (*corrubita lagenaria*) often used for booths and trellises in the Near East. Kent suggests that the word for plant used here is Egyptian, and that this may indicate that the writer was a Jew in dispersion living in Alexandria.[19] The question of course arises as to the need for the plant since Jonah had already built a booth. The trellis or vine, however, would make the booth more comfortable. The writer makes a major point of emphasizing Jonah's delight in his own comfort while he waits for Nineveh to suffer. In this sense the plant introduces a masterful touch. Also it is possible that the booth, being made of broken branches and leaves, would dry up quickly and not afford good shade.

Exceedingly glad: The satire of the writer is again at its best. Jonah is "exceedingly displeased" when the heathen are given a chance to enjoy life (4:1). He is "exceedingly glad" when he is himself given a chance to enjoy life.

4:7. *It withered:* The plant that brought joy to Jonah is destroyed by a worm. Again Jonah pouts. He is totally insensitive to the Ninevites on whom he wishes to inflict untold suffering, and totally sensitive to his own smallest discomfort. Jonah is capable of compassion—but the compassion is only for himself. We can gauge our maturity by the nature of our sensitivity. When we are more sensitive to ourselves and our needs than to others' needs, our immaturity shows. The more sensitive we are to the needs of others, the more mature we are.

4:8. *It is better for me to die:* Again Jonah asks to die. But this time the reason is different. A short time before (4:3) he wanted to die because God refused to inflict torture and destruction on the Ninevites. But now he wants to die when even a little discomfort—not torture, only a little discomfort—is inflicted upon himself. A better picture of an overgrown spoiled child cannot be found anywhere.

4:9. *Do you do well to be angry?* Jonah's petty selfishness, his blind prejudice and his violent reactions form a fitting backdrop for the superb expression of God's gentleness. God even shows mercy toward Jonah! How hard this must have been! Jonah is amazed and angered at God's showing mercy to the wicked Ninevites. But the far greater marvel is that God can still show mercy toward Jonah. Jonah thinks that the Ninevites are on trial. But the one on trial is Jonah. If anyone should be destroyed, it is he.

4:10. *You pity the plant:* Jonah's compassion for the plant stands in stark contrast to his lack of compassion for the people. God has maneuvered Jonah into a trap. He now drives home his message with great effectiveness. Jonah at the end is left speechless.

4:11. *Should I not pity Nineveh?* With these words God makes his point explicit. Even though Jonah has grown completely irrational, God persists in using calm logic. The argument is that Jonah, who feels pity for a mere plant on which he has bestowed no labor whatever (he did not even plant it), should be able to understand God's compassion for thousands of people on whom he has bestowed years and years of patient toil and loving affection.

Persons who do not know their right hand from their left: This expression does not necessarily mean children, as age is not specified. However, this seems to this writer to be what was intended, and many scholars have interpreted it the same way. One hundred twenty thousand children would indicate that the city's population was probably at least a half million.

Cattle: Animals in general.

Footnotes

[1] George M. Landes has pointed out (in unpublished discussions with the author) that the Hebrew word translated "overthrown" is ambiguous. He suggests that the author of *Jonah* may have deliberately used a word that can also mean "transformed." Jonah intended the former, but the Ninevites perceived the possibility of the latter.

[2] U.S. Department of Agriculture, Agricultural Stabilization and Conservation Service, *Commodity Credit Corporation Charts* (Washington: November 1972), p. 9.

[3] Norman J. Faramelli, *Technethics* (New York: Friendship Press, 1971), p. 97.

[4] *Oxford Economic Atlas of the World,* Fourth Edition, ed. D. B. Jones (London: Oxford University Press, 1972), p. 77.

[5] Barbara Ward, *The Lopsided World* (New York: W. S. Norton, 1968), pp. 106-107.

[6] At this point figures in Ward, *The Lopsided World,* pp. 106-107 are compared with figures taken from the *1973 Britannica Book of the Year* (Chicago: University of Chicago Press, 1973), p. 353.

[7] Faramelli, *op. cit.,* p. 84.

[8] *1973 Britannica Book of the Year,* p. 353.

[9] Barbara Ward, *op. cit.*, p. 12.

[10] Title of book by Barbara Ward cited above in footnote 5.

[11] *1973 Britannica Book of the Year*, p. 353.

[12] Faramelli, *op. cit.*, p. 94.

[13] *Ibid.*, p. 90.

[14] The reader is referred to the pamphlet, *International Development Strategy for the Second Development Decade*. It is a statement adopted by the United Nations General Assembly, October 1970, and may be secured from Department of State, Agency for International Development, Information Staff, Room 4898, Washington, D.C. 20523.

[15] K. M. Panikkar, *Asia and Western Dominance* (London: George Allen and Unwin, Ltd., 1955), pp. 424-425.

[16] "Whose Congo?," *International Review of Missions*, Vol. 50, No. 3 (July 1961), p. 273.

[17] *Ibid.* Also confirmed personally to the writer by a missionary to the Congo.

[18] *Interpreter's Bible*, ed. Nolan B. Harmon (New York: Abingdon Press, 1956), Vol. VI, p. 875. (Scarlett quotes from Clifford Bax's poem, "Turn Back O Man").

[19] Charles Foster Kent, *The Sermons, Epistles and Apocalypses of Israel's Prophets* (New York: Charles Scribner's Sons, 1910), p. 419.

STUDENT AND TEACHER AIDS

STUDY GUIDE

Introduction

Chapter V closed with an if: "if men only would, if men only could . . ." Are we to settle for an "If"? The day of ifs has past. The day of action has come. But action presupposes motivation and motivation presupposes learning. When is something learned? It is learned when it is lived; it is lived when it is assimilated into the thinking and practice of the learner.

Studying the Bible can only be a learning experience, therefore, if the biblical message is seen in terms of our daily lives. The Bible is a sacred book, but not merely a sacred book; it is also a book of flesh and blood. The flesh and blood—the live characters with loves and hates and passions and dreams like ours—must step out of the printed page and live with us if God's word, spoken centuries ago, is to speak again in our day.

This study book, which is focused on Jonah, is, therefore, also focused on you and me and on the issues of our day. Its primary concern is to promote personal growth and to motivate action. Each teacher in using the book should seek to develop a plan that will involve all participants at those levels of personal life where decisions are made and motivations are formed. The teacher's role is to provide for genuine learning experiences.

The first and most important initial involvement is for each student to read the study book. The book is written for the student, not the teacher. It is written in easy to read, non-technical language and the style is designed specifically to challenge the student. It is focused on the student's involvement and reflection in the face of contemporary issues. Students who read the book will, we believe, find the study coming alive. Hopefully they will be intrigued by the message of *Jonah* and by the way it unfolds.

This study guide provides for five sessions with additional teaching techniques and suggestions to enlarge the study as needed. If a Sunday School class should wish to use the study for a quarter (thirteen sessions) there is ample material for this purpose. The study plan has been worked out as a cooperative project by a group in Montgomery, Alabama, whose names appear in the acknowledgments. The guide is also indebted to the *National Teacher Education Project Manual*[1] prepared by Dr. Locke E. Bowman and to the book by Sara Little, *Learning Together in the Christian Fellowship*.[2] There are three steps in developing each session.

First, the teacher or leader should determine the goals of the session and identify the concepts that are to be dealt with. A concept is defined by Dr. Bowman as "a general idea that is capable of being constantly revised."[3] Learning involves revising our concepts, and revising concepts is an important part of this study. For example, we will note in Chapter I that our concept of the book of *Jonah* needs revising. In turn the book of *Jonah* is seen by some today as an attempt to help Israel revise her concept of mission. Revision of concepts will also play an important role as we take a new look at—as we "re-vision"—our mission today. In setting forth the goals for each session, the teacher will first determine the overall purpose of the session and then state the specific things for the students to accomplish. These objectives will be concrete things to be done by the students, not by the teacher, and will be stated in specific terms, not to oversimplify, but to make clear that if one is to grapple with issues in an understanding and creative way, one needs facts.

Second, the teacher needs to gain a personal knowledge of the resources available for the session. This is extremely important. The first requirement in this study is to become thoroughly familiar with the story of Jonah in the Bible and with the study book, commentaries, maps, audiovisuals available and any other resources. (See Bibliography.) In addition, the teacher should look for and develop local resources. Local groups can make posters, charts, banners and other visual aids. Also, almost every community has people who can serve as resource persons. For example, a teacher of economics or a businessman might discuss issues of economic injustice in the world; a returned G.I. or someone else who has been overseas might discuss issues related to the countries where he or she has been.

Third, the teacher needs to determine the means that will be used for communication and involvement. There are three steps in this third part of the study plan. First, the teacher decides on a way to begin. There are many possibilities, and the teacher should be creative and innovative. One suggestion is given in the main part of each of the sessions outlined below, and others are given in the supplementary guide for expanding the study. The second step is for the teacher to determine ways to sustain interest. The third step is to decide a way to conclude, including looking ahead to the next session. For any students who do not have copies of the study book it would be well for the teacher to provide typed or mimeographed copies of the objectives for the next session.

It should be remembered also that the first task of the teacher at each session is to create a relaxed, friendly, trusting atmosphere in which even the most timid will feel free to participate. The study of *Jonah* raises issues on which there will be differences of opinion. These differences need to be discussed in an atmosphere of openness, with mutual trust and respect even when opinions differ sharply. In such an atmosphere growth can take place and learning be actualized. The group working with the writer on this study guide suggested that the most effective way to create a good atmosphere for study is to open with worship. We recommend that each session open with a brief but well-planned devotional. Likewise it is good to close each session with a brief closing worship, which may at times consist only of a prayer.

The study book is divided into five chapters with each chapter built around an important concept related to the experience of Jonah. The theme of each chapter and the concepts it embodies will be explained in more detail in the guide for that chapter. The book also follows the text of *Jonah* verse by verse. The chapters, except for Chapter I, are divided into sections built around a verse or group of verses of *Jonah*. This has an advantage and a disadvantage. The advantage is that it makes the study experience-centered rather than topic-centered. The study follows the experiences of Jonah and allows the story to speak as we believe the author of *Jonah* intended it to speak. This means that each chapter has a variety of themes and emphases and enjoys all the advantages that variety affords. The disadvantage, however, is that the study is more difficult to organize. The study reflects life, and life does not come in neat, well-organized, logically constructed packages. Life has many facets, all showing at the same time. The study guide selects certain main themes and organizes study around them. The students and the teacher, however, should feel free to emphasize those facets of the study which appeal to them most and which are most relevant to their needs. The sectional divisions make it easy to expand the study into more than five sessions. The longer study can cover the material more thoroughly and can increase the breadth and depth of involvement.

Session I
The WORD

Chapter I gives a general introduction to *Jonah,* deals with popular misunderstandings of the book and sets forth in summary fashion the findings of biblical scholarship. It looks at the historical setting, examines the message of the book for the day in which it was written and suggests how the book is the "Word of the LORD" not only for ancient Israel, but also for our own age. It claims that *Jonah* is a missionary treatise in the finest sense of this term and lifts out the seven basic truths which *Jonah* sets forth as the "Word of the LORD" for our day.

A. Goals For This Session

1. Overall Purpose.

To achieve an understanding of the "Word of the LORD" that comes to us through the book of *Jonah* by clarifying and revising our concepts of the book in terms of:

    a. Popular misunderstandings of *Jonah;*
    b. The literary character and style of the book;
    c. The historical setting in which the book was written;
    d. The basic message of the book.

2. Specific Objectives.

This first session will probably be best presented in lecture form, with class participation as indicated below. If lecture is used, the specific objective in the session will be for the students to be able to restate in summary fashion the basic content of the chapter. The aim is not merely to master content, but to gain the knowledge needed in order to understand important issues and relate to them creatively. As a specific objective the students should be able at the end of the session to answer the questions listed at the end of Chapter I. These questions will be used in the study session as indicated below.

B. Relevant Resources

Bible, study book, commentaries, maps of Palestine during reign of Jeroboam II (786-741 B.C.) and post-exilic Israel (after 538 B.C.)

C. Suggestions For Communication and Involvement
1. Way to Begin.

There are many ways to begin the first session of a study. As noted above, creating an atmosphere of informality and establishing rapport are extremely important. A good way to begin this study on *Jonah* is to distribute blank sheets of paper and pencils. Ask each student to write down all the facts he knows about *Jonah*. When this is done, have the group share these facts. This exercise will probably show that most of us know little more than that Jonah was "swallowed by a whale" and then went to Nineveh. Explain that the first session will be primarily a lecture with discussion to follow. Students are to concentrate on content with a view to understanding the basic message of *Jonah*. Give out copies of the questions listed at the end of this chapter and ask the students to write down the answers as they hear them in the lecture. This makes students active participants in the entire session, since they have specific things to listen for. They will also participate more actively in the discussion period that follows the lecture.

2. Interaction to Sustain Interest.

When the lecture is finished, give the students a few minutes to complete their answers to the questions you have given them. Then have different members of the class read their answers. You might wish to use the chalkboard at this point to list answers, or you might find it more effective simply to discuss the answers as they are given, allowing each student to make a contribution in order to bring out the many facets of the message of *Jonah*.

If there is time, another project would be to divide the class into two groups—the Universalists and the Nationalists. Have the Universalists read *Isaiah* 42:1-9; 45:1-13; 49:1-6; 60:3; and 66:18-23. Have the Nationalists read the book of *Nahum, Nehemiah* 9:26-10, and 13:23-30 and *Ezra* 10. Then have group one present the Universalists' understanding of Israel's mission, and group two in turn present the Nationalists' understanding of Israel's mission.

3. A Way to Conclude—Looking Ahead.

The teacher can summarize the insights gained from the discussion of the questions, and can identify the author of the book with the Universalists and Jonah with the Nationalists. Assign Chapter II for Session II and ask the students to look for pictures, newspaper or magazine articles, and other materials related to the theme of rebellion and bring them to class. Suggest that the students come prepared to discuss the questions that appear at the end of each section in Chapter II. Appoint a leader for each of the three work groups that will function during Session II. Meet with these leaders to explain their responsibilities.

For Expanded Study

In an expanded study we suggest that the teacher still cover Chapter I in the first session, since the method is lecture. If there is need of more discussion, an additional session may be used. However, since Chapter I provides the basis for the rest of the study, each session will be referring back to it in one way or another, and for this reason one session on the chapter should be adequate.

Session II
Rebel

Chapter II deals with Jonah's call and his refusal to go to Nineveh. It focuses especially on Jonah's name, "Jonah, son of Amittai," applying the symbolical meaning of the name both to ancient Israel and to our day. It looks at Jonah's flight to Tarshish in terms of contemporary rebellions against God. It shows that though we may defy God, we cannot escape Him.

A. Goals For This Session

1. Overall Purpose.

To study Jonah's call and his rebellion as a clue to an understanding of our own call and our own rebellion.

2. Specific Objectives.

At the end of the session the students should be able to:

a. State the symbolical meaning of Jonah's name and relate this name both to Israel and to our day, noting the contradiction between Jonah's name and his flight to Tarshish.

b. Compare Jonah's flight from God with the ways we run from God today.

c. Identify the attitudes and beliefs that caused Jonah to act the way he did and to give modern examples of the same attitudes and beliefs.

d. State ways in which both Jonah's rebellion and ours are rebellions that masquerade as obedience.

e. Compare the storm that thwarted Jonah's attempt to escape, with the storms that rage in our day.

f. List evidences that we cannot escape God and his moral laws for the universe.

B. Relevant Resources

Bible, Chapter II of study book, other books and commentaries, clippings from newspapers and magazines, television news reports and specials.

C. Suggestions for Communication and Involvement

1. A Way to Begin: Work Groups.

The teacher may wish to read *Jonah* 1:1-4 and lift out briefly for the class the meanings of words and phrases as stated in the exegesis in the study book. Then the class can be divided into three sub-groups, the leader for each group having been chosen at least a week ahead of time. The task of each group will be to study one of the three sections of this chapter for twenty to thirty minutes and to suggest answers to the questions found at the end of the section. Group one will study

"Jonah, Son of Amittai": God's Call; Group two: "Jonah Rose to Flee": Rebellion; Group three: "The Lord Hurled a Great Wind": The Impossibility of Escape.

2. Interaction to Sustain Interest.

Following the work group sessions the class will come together to discuss their findings and conclusions. A person designated by each group will make a brief report followed by questions and discussion. The teacher will keep before them the basic goal of the session and will seek to bring out not only the contribution of each group, but also of each student.

3. A Way To Conclude—Looking Ahead.

Have the leader of each subgroup make a summary statement, or if preferred, the teacher of the class can make this summary for all three sections. Then the teacher will point toward Chapter III, *Crisis,* and make assignments for the next session. Ask each student to bring in clippings from newspapers or magazines reflecting the crises and storms of our day as expressed in Chapter III of the study book.

For Expanded Study

In an expanded study the teacher and students will use the same objectives for Chapter II as stated above. However, the pursuit of these objectives can occupy two sessions, each session following the basic outline:

    A. Set the specific objectives for the session

    B. Become acquainted with relevant resources

    C. Determine methods for communication and involvement including a way to begin, interaction to sustain interest and a way to conclude.

Session one in the expanded study would deal with sections 1 and 2 of Chapter II: "Jonah, the Son of Amittai": God's Call and "Jonah Rose to Flee": Rebellion. A way to proceed would be to begin with the method of work groups and to follow the suggestions related to work groups as outlined above.

Session two would deal with section 3 of Chapter II, "The Lord Hurled a Great Wind": The Impossibility of Escape and would focus on the impossibility of escaping God. A good way to begin this session would be to use the technique of poetry analysis. Have a qualified person, preferably an English literature teacher, analyze the poem "The Hound of Heaven" in the context of Francis Thompson's life. The focus would be on his flight from God and the impossibility of escape. For example, what would "fled Him down the labyrinthine ways of my own mind" and "adown titanic glooms of chasmed fears" mean coming from an ex-drug addict? The analysis of the poem should open up a discussion of our attempts to escape God. Also the class might look for similarities between the poem and the story of Jonah. Use the questions listed at the end of each section.

Session III
Crisis

Chapter III focuses on the storm that resulted from Jonah's flight. It looks at the various events that transpired aboard ship and raises such contemporary issues as our own sleep in the midst of contemporary storms, our small concepts of God, our arrogant pride and our tendency toward heroics, as well as the question of how to preserve what is valid in a noble heritage when the clamor all about us demands constant change. It raises the issue of how to determine what should and what should not be changed. It raises the question of our motives for mission and points to the centrality of Christ as the only adequate motive in a world where many cultures and religions must live side by side.

A. Goals For This Session

1. Overall Purpose.

To enter into the crisis created by Jonah's rebellion by means of role play in order that we may identify the many ways in which our own rebellion against God has created a similar crisis in our day.

2. Specific Objectives.

This chapter contains a wide range of material. The following is a list of possible objectives for the students, things which they might be able to do at the end of the session. Since there is probably more in this chapter than can be covered in one session, the teacher will need to select those objectives which are most important for the local group and which are obtainable in one session:

a. State specific ways in which Jonah's sleeping through the storm is symbolic of what many Christians are doing today.

b. State ways in which our sleep as a church and as Christians has allowed injustice and denial of human dignity to continue.

c. State specifically how Jonah's god was too small, and show how this is often our problem today.

d. Show how the answer to the question "Of what people are you?" often determines a person's place in our communities.

e. Give specific suggestions as to how we might tear down the cultural, social, economic and racial barriers that divide people from people in our world.

f. Identify elements within our own culture that should not change and elements that should be changed or eliminated.

g. Identify ways in which we may use religion for personal advantage; identify unworthy motives for Christian mission.

h. Identify the heart of the Christian faith as the new creation in Christ and state what it means for Christians and non-Christians alike to come to the foot of the cross.

i. Suggest ways in which Christians and non-Christians may be allies and not enemies.

j. Suggest ways for Christian churches to work together more closely, looking toward greater unity in Christ in an ecumenical (worldwide) fellowship.

B. Relevant Resources

Bible, Chapter III in study book, clippings from newspapers and magazines, interviews with persons concerned with crisis situations.

C. Suggestions for Communication and Involvement

1. A Way to Begin: Role Play.

Role play is the brief acting out of a situation in which groups or individuals identify with other groups or individuals. The aim is for persons to understand how others feel. They take on themselves a particular point of view and try to reproduce the experiences of persons or groups. It is not a rehearsed drama with a prepared script. It is brief, usually lasts from three to ten minutes. In conducting the role play the teacher describes the situation, chooses the characters and lets them quickly structure the scene they will play. Characters needed in this role play are Jonah, the captain and the sailors.

The teacher may wish to read aloud the story of the storm in *Jonah* 1:4-16, lifting out briefly the meaning of some words and phrases as explained in the exegesis found in the study book. After reading the chapter the role play will proceed, lasting from five to ten minutes depending on the group.

2. Interaction to Sustain Interest.

As soon as the role play is over the teacher will help the class to analyze what took place. The characters and the class may share insights. The teacher can help the students identify the issues involved in the crisis by looking at relevant parts of exegesis and exposition and by raising some of the study questions found at the end of each section in Chapter III of the study book. The teacher will have in mind the questions that are most important in the local situation. Also the students can indicate the issues they feel are most important.

3. A Way To Conclude—Looking Ahead.

The teacher can summarize the session by focusing on our contemporary crisis and lifting up the issues that face us today. This will point the way to the urgency of repentance, and the teacher can assign Chapter IV on "Repentance" for the next session. It may be helpful to note that the crisis in *Jonah* fits into the following pattern:

(a) An incident or incidents precipitate a crisis. Conflicts of interest arise.

(b) Confusion results. Issues are unclear.

(c) There is an attempt to analyze and identify problems and place blame.

(d) Opposing forces defend points of view; persons at fault try to save face; attempts are made to find solutions that will resolve the crisis.

(e) Decisions are made; action is taken; and the crisis is resolved (though sometimes only temporarily, and the search for a more permanent solution continues).

111

An expanded study would spend considerable time on this, the longest chapter in the book. Such a study could involve four sessions, each session following the basic outline as already described.

Session one would cover section 1 of the chapter, "Jonah . . . Was Fast Asleep: Lethargy" and would use the role play technique as explained above.

Session two would cover section 2 of the chapter and center around our concept of God. A good technique would be a book review with forum. Have someone give a review of J. B. Phillip's book, *Your God Is Too Small*. After the review give the group an opportunity to ask the book reviewer questions. The teacher can reserve time to conclude with questions: "In what ways was Jonah's concept of God too small?" In what ways do we in a technological age have tribal gods?

Session three would cover sections 3 and 4 of Chapter III, "Of What People Are You?": Pride and "I Am a Hebrew": Heritage, and would focus on the issue of how we can hold to a valid heritage yet be humble and open to change. Here the technique of lecture with three listening groups could be used. The teacher would divide the class into three groups. Group one would be assigned to listen for ways in which Jonah's pride in being a Hebrew was a block to the fulfilling of God's purpose. Group two would listen for ways in which Jonah's pride in being a Hebrew was essential to the fulfillment of God's purpose. Group three would listen for clues as to how to distinguish today between what must be held on to as valid and essential in our heritage, and what must be changed or discarded as a block to the fulfillment of God's purpose.

Session four would deal with sections 5 and 6 of Chapter III, "Throw Me Into the Sea": Heroics and "Nevertheless, the Men Rowed Hard": Humanization. For beginning and sustaining interest the teacher could use the technique of circular response. This method works best when the group numbers not more than fifteen. So if your group is larger than fifteen, divide it. Members are seated in a circle. The teacher proposes a question to be taken up, which might be "What do you think was Jonah's motivation for becoming a martyr and a hero?" or "Why do you think the sailors rowed hard in order to save Jonah's life?" The discussion begins with the man or woman at the teacher's right. That person has the first opportunity to express his or her views. Then the next person to the right has a chance to talk and so on until the discussion has been around the circle. No member of the group can speak a second time until his or her turn comes again. After the teacher summarizes the viewpoints, then another question can be posed such as "How did Jonah show a condescending attitude toward the sailors?" After several questions have been dealt with in this fashion, the teacher may want to open up a general discussion and then lift out further issues for study.

Session IV
Repentance

Chapter IV looks at Jonah's trip to Nineveh, his preaching and the response of the people of Nineveh. It raises the question of how we may either consciously or unconsciously try to use God for our own purposes. The chapter points to what it calls the "subtle satisfactions of saving sinners." It discusses the repentance of the Ninevites and contrasts their humble attitude with the refusal of Jonah to see his own need for repentance. It raises the question of repentance in our day and suggests that the current "new humanism," a reaction to the pessimism of neo-orthodox theology, may be too shallow and unrealistic in its diagnosis of our contemporary crisis.

A. Goals For This Session

1. Overall Purpose.

To study God's call to repentance in the light of Jonah's reluctant mission to Nineveh and the response of the Ninevites.

2. Specific Objectives.

At the end of this session the students should be able to:

a. Contrast Jonah's approach to the Ninevites with the approach of Jesus to the sinners in his day, and to apply this comparison to the role of Christians in areas of tension created by injustice, oppression and denial of human dignity.

b. Contrast the repentance of the Ninevites with the unrepentant attitudes of Jonah.

c. Examine ways in which we may consciously or unconsciously seek to use God for our own ends.

d. State ways in which we need to repent today.

113

e. Examine ways in which God uses the church and Christians in mission, as he did Jonah, in spite of their shortcomings and lack of repentance.

B. Relevant Resources

Bible, Chapter IV in study book.

C. Suggestions for Communication and Involvement

1. A Way to Begin: Buzz Groups.

The teacher may wish to read *Jonah* 2:10-3:10, lifting out the meaning of any obscure words or phrases as found in the exegesis in the study book. The class will then be divided into buzz groups. Buzz groups allow a hundred percent participation by a large group through division into smaller subgroups. Six is the usual number in a buzz group, the method originally being called "Phillips 66" because a Dr. Phillips of Michigan State College started the practice of dividing an audience into groups of six for six minutes of discussion. The number in each buzz group for this session can range from three to six, depending on the size of the class. The teacher will write the following question (or another question pertinent to repentance) on the chalkboard: "In what ways does the church need to change?" The members of each group will be asked to discuss the question among themselves for five to ten minutes.

2. Interaction to Sustain Interest.

After the buzz groups are over and the class is called together, the teacher will ask each buzz group to report. Points may be noted on a chalkboard if desired. After the suggestions are listed, the teacher may inquire if the answers to the question imply repentance. Does the church need to repent? Do Christians need to repent? Here the teacher may point again to the content of Chapter IV making sure to stress the important ideas stated in the objectives for this session. This presentation should open the way for a general discussion of the questions found at the end of the sections.

3. A Way to Conclude—Looking Ahead.

The teacher may summarize the meaning of repentance in the words of *Jonah* 3:8: "Let everyone turn from his evil way," then pose the question: Did Jonah ever repent? Ask the class to read *Jonah* 4 for the next session with this question in mind.

Also assign Chapter V of the study book. In looking ahead, the teacher will be sure that the panel for Session V has been selected and that the participants all have the study book to read.

For Expanded Study

The expanded study for Chapter IV would include two sessions, each session following the basic outline already described. The first session would deal with sections 1 and 2, "And It Vomited out Jonah: Second Chance" and "Nineveh Shall Be Overthrown: Saving Sinners." A good method for this session would be conversation followed by discussion. After lifting up the objectives for the session and looking at the verses in the Bible together with the relevant exegesis in the study book, the teacher would ask persons in the group to discuss in pairs Jonah's motivation for going to Nineveh. After a short time of such informal discussion, the teacher calls the group back to order and asks for reports from each conversation team. As each team gives its idea of Jonah's motivation, the leader can list it on the chalkboard and call for discussion, always trying to bring the discussion to some conclusions bearing in mind the objectives for the session.

The second session would deal with section 3 of this chapter, "Let Everyone Turn": Repentance, and would use the technique of buzz groups stated above, the focus being on repentance.

Session V
Mission

Chapter V centers around *Jonah* 4:1-11 and focuses on Jonah's reaction to God's forgiveness of the Ninevites. It shows Jonah as the most rebellious, the most obstinate and the most unyielding character of the entire Bible. Jonah defies God: he tries to order God around; and when God will not yield to his pressure he peevishly says, "It is better for me to die." This chapter brings out Jonah's self-indulgent concern for himself and his complete unconcern for the people of Nineveh. It also brings out his desire to die rather than to accept the Ninevites as God's children. Yet, God has the last word, and the closing verse of *Jonah* expresses the limitless love of God both in scope and in depth of tenderness.

115

A. Goals For This Session

1. Overall Purpose.

To examine the Christian mission in today's world in the light of our failures, as reflected in the book of *Jonah,* and in the light of the challenge of God's all-inclusive love, as also reflected in the book of *Jonah.*

2. Specific Objectives.

At the end of the session the students should be able to:

a. State why God's forgiveness of the Ninevites made Jonah so angry.

b. State why issues of race are so explosive.

c. State the meaning of the phrase "Rather die than live" as expressed in the study book.

d. State evidences of the increase or decrease of prejudice, and the increase or decrease of injustice in their community.

e. State the basic causes of racial and national tensions that keep our contemporary world on the brink of bloody conflict.

f. Show how Jonah, concerned over his own comfort and oblivious to the needs of the Ninevites, symbolizes our modern world where many of us likewise put "plants" above people.

g. State the facts of our lopsided world in which a few people live in extreme wealth and the masses live in extreme poverty, and explain something of the complications of world economic structures that produce these conditions.

h. Point out how Jonah's unyielding hatred of Nineveh left him alone on the hillside while God's love is triumphant in spite of Jonah's refusal to change.

B. Relevant Resources

Bible; study book, Chapter V; pamphlets relating data on poverty, distribution of wealth, and other economic data; the United Methodist Social Creed.

C. Suggestions for Communication and Involvement

1. A Way to Begin: Panel Discussion.

The teacher may wish to read Chapter 4 of *Jonah* and refer to the exegesis for any words or phrases that need a brief explanation. An excellent way to begin this session would be to ask persons knowledgeable in areas of mission concern to form a panel. You might select a teacher of economics or foreign affairs, a businessman or a banker, a social worker, a congressman or legislator, a lawyer or other person knowledgeable in civil rights and a minister. The panel should not have more than three or four persons. In some communities resource persons may be few, but oftentimes we are surprised at the number we can find when we look around. The members of the panel would be asked to read the last chapter in the study book (preferably the entire book) and be prepared to discuss the issues raised. For the first thirty to forty-five minutes the class would listen to the panel discussion, the teacher serving as moderator and asking them questions.

2. Interaction to Sustain Interest.

An open forum can follow the panel discussion, with members of the class asking questions of the panel members. This can be done either by writing the questions and handing them to the moderator or by asking questions directly from the floor.

3. A Way to Conclude—Looking Ahead.

It is most likely that this session will raise more questions than it answers, and some effort should be made to direct each student toward a decision to do something about his or her own repentance and mission. A closing worship service for the whole study along this line would be most appropriate. The "looking ahead" for this session is not looking ahead to another session, but looking ahead to involvement and action.

For Expanded Study

For expanded study, Chapter V would be divided into four sessions corresponding to the four sections of the chapter. Each session would follow the basic outline already described.

Session one, "Better for Me to Die," could use the technique of brainstorming, a term coined by Alex Osborn in "Your Creative Power." [4] In this procedure rules of judgment are suspended if only temporarily. A problem is posed and for ten to fifteen minutes the group is asked to put forward all the ideas they have. The ideas are recorded without comment and especially without criticism. In this session the question might be: Why did Jonah become so angry at God for sparing the

Ninevites? After the fun of being able to be spontaneous, the group can settle down to serious study. Often the brainstorming opens suggestions that can be followed seriously with great profit. The teacher can draw attention to the section of the study book itself and to the questions listed at the end of the section.

Session two, "Jonah . . . Made A Booth For Himself," might use the technique of the simulation game. There are elaborate games available from various sources. In this session we suggest you build your own brief, informal one. It will go something like this: Give each person a number as he or she arrives. Numbers will run from 1-3. There will be only two number 1's, four number 2's, and the rest will be number 3's. (In case the group is quite large, you might have three or four number 1's and six or eight number 2's. If the group is very small, use only two numbers with one or two number 1's and the rest number 2's. In this case the number 2's are treated as number 3's.)

The groups will meet in separate parts of the room. Crowd all number 3's into the smallest corner, requiring them to stand because there is not enough space and not enough money for chairs. Give big, ample space to number 1's, furnishing them with big comfortable chairs. For about ten or fifteen minutes the teacher will completely ignore the number 3's and concentrate attention on the number 1's with a little attention to 2's. The teacher and the number 1's and 2's will make slighting, derogatory remarks about the number 3's as being lazy, shiftless, illiterate and uncultured. They may use national or racial slurs in referring to them. The teacher will have arranged for some nice refreshments to be served, but when the refreshments come in, the 1's will gorge themselves, the number 2's receive an ample serving, but the number 3's will be completely ignored. They will have to stand in their crowded corner and watch the 1's and 2's enjoy themselves. Then when the 1's and 2's have feasted, the 3's will finally be shown a little attention by being required to clean up the mess created by the 1's and 2's.

Do not reveal to the group in the beginning the purpose of the game or how it is played. Let them find out as you proceed so that they will experience their respective roles. The wealthiest people in the group should be placed in the number 3 group and the poorest in the number 1 group. Then after the simulation play, the teacher will point out that the 3's represent about 75 percent of the world's population, while the 1's represent around 5 percent, and 2's around 20 percent. The teacher will then ask questions about how the various people felt. For example, how did the 3's feel when the 1's and 2's ate all the refreshments? How did the 1's and 2's feel eating with the hungry 3's looking on? How did the 3's feel standing while the 1's sat in comfort? How did they feel when required to clean up? The discussion of these questions can lead to a fruitful discussion of the questions at the end of this section in the study book. The teacher and group will find that they can be imaginative and creative in using this method. Add flourishes, new elements and make the game your own.

Session three, "You Pity the Plant": Callousness, could use the technique of a panel discussion followed by a forum as described above, only that the focus of the panel if used in this extended study would be on section 3 alone rather than on the entire chapter.

Session four, "And Also Much Cattle": Love, would lift up the stark contrast between Jonah's unyielding hate and God's unlimited love. This might be done in a number of ways. One way would be to use the study question at the end of chapter V. Each student might write down an imaginary scene with a conversation between God and Jonah, or the class might be divided into groups of twos or fours with the members of each group verbally suggesting to the others their imaginary scenes until the group has developed one together. The leader might suggest the many possibilities and give a model to stimulate the use of creative imagination. Such a model might be:

Jonah and God are seated together in the now unshaded booth. God speaks: "Can't you understand, Jonah? These are my children! I love every one of them."

Jonah, fuming, retorts, "Your children, bah! What do you mean, your children? They're nothing but Ninevites! We Israelites are your children."

God, in a patient but firm voice, replies, "Jonah, I know every one of them by name. You can see that they are sorry for their sin. How can I destroy them? Take these field glasses, Jonah, and look closely. See the little crippled boy over there with the big broad grin on his face? Yes, that's the one standing near the red cow. His name is Ashurbanipal. The boys call him Bani. He can't run like the others, but when there's a ball game, he's always there rooting for his team.

"And see Larsa over there, Jonah? See that look on his face? You'd recognize it anywhere. Watch him glancing at Ishtar out of the corner of his eye and notice the shy look on Ishtar's face. Now turn your field glasses down toward the river. See the little girl holding a rag doll. Her name is Shamra. Her father gave her the doll and she takes it with her everywhere she goes. Jonah, did you ever see a little girl sound asleep with a dirty rag doll cuddled up to a chubby cheek? Jonah, these are my children!"

It is obvious that Jonah has become more and more irritated. He is now furious. God will not bow to his pressure. He rises, throws the field glasses on the ground in disgust, and turns his back abruptly to make clear his defiance of this weakling, sentimental God who will neither vindicate his prophet nor prove that he is God. As he turns he spits out something which sounds like, "Your children, h . . .! They're nothing but d . . . Ninevites!"

God speaks no more. As he turns to go he looks back at Jonah with sad but patient eyes, and then makes his way down into Nineveh where he has much forgiving to take care of. Jonah stands for a long time motionless, staring into the distance as if he sees or hears nothing. He is hardly aware that God has walked away and left him. But he feels a deep sense of emptiness, a sense of having been deserted. He remains silent, in a daze. Slowly his lips move as though they unconsciously reflect the anguish of his soul: God is dead!

Suddenly a cow lows in the distance. The familiar sound brings Jonah back to mundane reality—the only reality remaining in a world where God is dead. Immediately his thoughts turn again to his own comfort. He bends down over the sprig of the withered plant, tenderly stirs the soil around it with his index finger, and carefully waters it with fresh cool water from his drinking flask.

This session four in the expanded study could also include a review of the basic message of *Jonah* using the seven point outline found in Chapter I of the study book, asking the students to appraise the entire study. Questions that needed further study could be discussed. Also the question of what can we do specifically to express our new sense of mission could engage the attention of the group. The following experience of a missionary might provide stimulation for discussion of mission wherever we are:

Although I felt I was following God's will for my life when I left home to go as a young missionary to a foreign field, it was not easy. The ties with my parents, sisters and brothers were very strong. The thought of five years of separation brought a lump in my throat. Some people said to me, "This must take a great deal of courage." But I knew I had the backing and support of my family as well as my church. I was sent away on wings of prayer. In a non-Christian country it was not surprising that the missionaries and national Christians did not receive the full backing of the government, which was even unfriendly at times. But from home I received regular letters of encouragement and assurances of prayers. There were also expressions of pride and joy that I was representing them on this foreign mission field.

War conditions brought me back to the States. Because of my deep concern in the area of race relations in the United States, God led me to work in a home mission agency of our church, a community center in a black neighborhood, with a biracial staff. Never had I faced a greater challenge or felt that I was participating in a work that was more needed than sharing life with this staff as we tried to bring new life and understanding, in the name of Christ, to the people of this neighborhood. I felt a sense of oneness with my co-workers as I had on the foreign field.

However, I realized very soon that many of the folks in my home town and state were not interested in my life here and what we were trying to do. At first I noticed a "coolness" and this disappointed me. Then from people I least expected came expressions of real opposition to my being associated with this type of work. They seemed

121

embarrassed that this was my choice. This hurt me deeply. To realize that people whom I loved and in whom I had confidence had such deep prejudices toward some of God's children caused my heart to ache more than it ever had in that foreign land. In a foreign land we sometimes expected opposition from non-Christians, but in the United States to receive criticism and distrust from church people caused me great distress.

It took a different kind of courage to continue in this work of race relations, to learn to love and not to judge, and to try to gently help people to have more understanding and acceptance of people of other races.

When I felt in my heart that what I was doing was God's will for me and I trusted Him for strength, I am grateful that I found that *His grace was sufficient.*

(This statement could be used in one of the five basic sessions if the group is not following the expanded session.)

Footnotes

[1] Locke E. Bowman, Jr., Donald L. Griggs, Donald P. McGuirk, *National Teacher Education Project Manual* (The Arizona Experiment, 6947 East Mac-Donald Dr., Scottsdale, Arizona, 1970).

[2] Sara Little, *Learning Together in the Christian Fellowship* (Richmond: John Knox Press, 1958).

[3] Bowman, *op. cit.*, section C-1.

[4] Taken from *New Hope for Audiences* (Chicago: National Congress of Parents and Teachers, 1954), p. 12.

APPENDIX I
Authorship, Dating and Style

For a long time the commonly held view was that Jonah, the prophet of Jeroboam's reign, wrote the book of *Jonah*. However, this seems unlikely for a number of reasons. First, when we read the book we discover that it is a book about Jonah and not by him. There is no indication anywhere that Jonah was himself the author. Unlike *Jeremiah, Amos, Micah* and *Hosea* and other prophetic books written by the prophets whose names they bear, the book always refers to Jonah in the third person. In this regard it is similar to *Ruth, Esther* and *Job.* When the author quotes Jonah he is careful to indicate that he is quoting, which shows that the author was not himself the historical Jonah.

Furthermore, one will note that the book is the only one of the so called "twelve minor prophets" that is cast throughout in narrative form, except of course for the psalm in chapter two. Other prophetic books such as *Amos* and *Hosea* relate some of the experiences of the prophets, but the books themselves are composed mainly of prophetic utterances. *Jonah,* on the other hand, is simply a story about the prophet Jonah, There is a complete absence of all prophetic discourse (unless the psalm in chapter two be considered as such, which is hardly possible). Jonah speaks only eight words as a prophet (five in the Hebrew text). What we have in *Jonah* is not a prophetic discourse thundered forth after the manner of an Amos or a Micah, but rather the story of a prophet who rebelled against God.

Likewise, it should be noted that the entire narrative is in the past tense. This indicates that the writer was recording events that had happened before his time, and would date the writing after the eighth century B.C. Opinion is divided as to exactly when after the eighth century it was written, but the majority

123

of scholars in recent years have dated the writing after the exile (586 B.C.-538 B.C.). Some scholars at present are suggesting that it may be pre-exilic in origin.[1] The expression in 3:3, "Now Nineveh was a large city," could mean that the city was large when Jonah visited it, or it could indicate that the city was no longer in existence when the author was writing. In the former case, the date of writing could have been anytime after the eighth century and thus could have been before the exile. In the latter case the writing would have been after 612 B.C., the date that Nineveh was destroyed and thus could still have been before the exile, which began in 586 B.C. For a number of reasons, however, as indicated in this appendix, many scholars to the present time date the book after the exile.

In the same manner, the reference to the size of Nineveh in 3:3 as being "three days journey in breadth" [2] points to a date later than the eighth century when the historical Jonah lived, and probably to a date sometime after the destruction of Nineveh. Considering that the average person can walk fifteen to twenty-five miles a day, a three-days journey would be from forty-five to seventy-five miles. However, archeological excavations reveal that Nineveh proper was only approximately seven and one-half miles in circumference. Archeologist F. Jones states its size as follows: east wall, 16,000 ft. (3.03 miles); north wall, 7,000 ft. (1.32 miles); west wall, 13,600 ft. (2.57 miles); south wall, 3,000 ft. (1.56 miles).[3] Long after Nineveh was destroyed, however, the name *Nineveh* came to be used by many to designate not just the original walled city, but a much larger area. *Genesis* 10:11-12 includes Rehobeth-Ir, Resen and Calah along with Nineveh in what it calls "the great city," the same expression used in *Jonah* 1:2. Jones estimates that this "greater Nineveh" would have comprised a circuit of about 61 miles. Thus, the expression "three days journey in breadth" is quite understandable if the book was written around 500 B.C. or later.

Another indication of a late date for the composition of the book is the reference to the "king of Nineveh" in 3:6. A person writing during the time of Jonah (c. 800-750 B.C.) would most likely have said "King of Assyria." Eiselen points out that "this title [King of Nineveh] could never have been applied to the kings of Assyria while the Assyrian empire was still in existence," and states "this conclusion is supported by the exhaustive study of Professor Wilson of the titles of the Assyrian kings found in the inscriptions and in the Old Testament." [4] Landes contends that this is not decisive, pointing out that, "The pattern 'king of (name of city)' is found elsewhere in the OT in the expressions 'king of Salem' (Gen. 14:18), 'king of Gerar' (Gen. 20:2), 'king of Arad' (Num. 21:1), 'king of Jericho' (Josh. 2:2), and 'king of Samaria' (I Kgs. 21:1)— all in pre-exilic texts.' " [5] However, this argument hardly seems to answer Eiselen's contention. All the kings mentioned by Landes were seemingly small potentates, not kings of a vast empire. Also what applies in one case would not necessarily apply in another. Eiselen and Wilson contend specifically that the King of Assyria would not have been spoken of as "King of Nineveh" during the lifetime of the Assyrian Empire.

There are also a number of passages in the book of *Jonah* which parallel closely passages in other Old Testament books that are of post-exilic origin. *Jonah* 3:9 is similar to *Joel* 2:14. *Jonah* 4:2b refers to God's self-disclosure in the covenant with Israel as recorded in *Exodus* 34:6. Parallels to *Exodus* 34:6 are found in *Joel* 2:13, *Psalms* 86:15, and *Psalms* 103:8. The psalm in *Jonah* 2:2-9 has numerous parallels in the book of *Psalms*. For details see exegesis following chapter 4. These parallels are quite striking. As Eiselen points out, they "cannot be due to accident." [6] Either the writer of *Jonah* was familiar with the psalms and quoted them as did Jesus on a number of occasions, or else the author of the various psalms was familiar with Chapter II of *Jonah*. The former seems much more likely and, though it certainly cannot point to any precise date, does indicate a late date for the book's composition.

One should also note that Chapter II is a psalm of thanksgiving *after* deliverance: "Yet thou didst bring up my life from the pit." The deliverance has already been accomplished. As noted in the exegesis on page 70, the psalm seems to have originated as a hymn of thanksgiving after some remarkable deliverance. It is an "ode to liberation." Verse four, "Then I said, 'I am cast out from thy presence; how shall I look again upon thy holy temple?' " and verse seven, "When my soul fainted within me, I remembered the Lord; and my prayer came to thee, into thy holy temple," allude to separation from the temple. Worship was not centralized in Jerusalem until Josiah's reform in 621 B.C. just prior to the exile and more than a hundred years after the time of the historical Jonah. The author of *Jonah* uses the psalm because it fits his purpose of depicting Israel through the experience of Jonah. Verse 2:8, "Those who pay regard to vain idols forsake their true loyalty," alludes to the Israelites who were weak and succumbed to idol worship. The expression in verse three, "All thy waves and thy billows passed over me" is a direct quotation from *Psalms* 42:7, which psalm is an outcry of one who is separated from the temple. The psalm is usually associated with the exile, and certainly dates after 621 when worship was centralized in the temple.

The psalm in Chapter II, then, and other quotations or references in *Jonah* seem to indicate a post-exilic date for the writing of the book. Since the exile ended around 538 B.C., the date of the writing of *Jonah* would appear to be after this date. Whether the book was written before or after the exile, however, the facts at least seem to point to the conclusion that it was not written during the lifetime of the historical Jonah. This in no way affects the place of the book in scripture or its inspiration as the word of God. The fact that at one time some supposed the eighth century B.C. prophet to have been the author was due to the mistaken notion that the person whose name a book bears must have written the book. As is seen in the case of such books as *Ruth*, *Job* and *Esther*, this is not necessarily true and in no way affects the inspiration of the book. In fact, a large number of books in the Old Testament are anonymous. Though tradition has assigned authors to some of them, the books themselves do not say who wrote them. *Jonah*, as far as authorship is concerned, should have been classified with these writings rather than with *Amos*, *Hosea*, *Micah* and *Isaiah*. For the story clearly is a story about Jonah in exactly the same way as the books of *Ruth*, *Esther* and *Job* are stories about these persons.

The question of whether the writing of *Jonah* was pre-exilic or post-exilic must remain an open one for the present. Contrary to the majority opinion of scholars in the twentieth century, Landes presents cogent arguments for dating the book before the exile.[7] It is not our purpose in this study to enter into this debate. For our purposes a post-exilic or pre-exilic date makes little difference since the message is the same in either case. Though the exclusivistic policies of Judaism reached their peak in the post-exilic period, they by no means are absent before the exile. As indicated elsewhere in these pages, hatred of Israel's oppressors, particularly the Assyrians, was certainly intense in the seventh and eighth centuries B.C. So the call to repentance and to a change of attitude toward the Gentile world as a key to the understanding of Israel's mission in the world could have originated prior to the exile as well as after. It seems likely to the present writer that the book originated in the post-exilic period, and so we deal with it on this assumption. Certainly it spoke to the conditions of the post-exilic age in a special way, given the reforms of Ezra and the growth of extreme exclusivistic tendencies. It is the present writer's opinion that the book originated sometime between 500 B.C. and 300 B.C., probably soon after the reform movement of Ezra in 397 B.C.

Footnotes

[1] George M. Landes, Union Theological Seminary, New York, New York, in an unpublished manuscript and in correspondence with the author.

[2] George Landes points out that the expression "three days" or "three days and three nights" was a familiar motif in ancient Israel, and that it was not always used in a strictly literal sense. ("The 'Three Days and Three Nights' Motif in Jonah 2:1," *Journal of Biblical Literature*, December 1967, pp. 446-450.

[3] F. Jones, "Topography of Nineveh," *Journal of the Royal Asian Society*, XV, 1855, p. 556.

[4] Eiselen, F. C., *The Minor Prophets* (New York: Eaton and Mains, 1907), p. 335.

[5] George Landes in unpublished correspondence with the author.

[6] Eiselen, *op. cit.*

[7] Landes, in unpublished correspondence with the author.

APPENDIX II
Historicity

Some will want to raise the question of the historicity of
Jonah in more detail than we have done in the preceding
pages—particularly the fish incident. Though it is the kind of
question that is difficult to deal with, the following facts and
considerations may be helpful.

First, we should recognize that there is no means of proving
the issue one way or the other from a scientific point of view.
The answer in final analysis will be determined by what we
believe about it.

Second, there is no inherent reason why the incident could
not be literal history. To say that it could not have happened,
however scientific and sound such a claim may seem to be
from the modern scientific point of view, is in fact to be un-
scientific. It is to fall victim to scientific positivism or dogmatism.

Third, the truthfulness, the inspiration and the authority of
the Bible are not at stake in this issue. Those who believe
that we should understand the story as literal history have a
clearly defensible position from the point of view of faith, since
Christians do not question that all things are possible with God.
Likewise, those who believe that the incident should not be
understood as literal history have an equally defensible position from the point of view of faith, as we will seek to show.
It should be stressed that neither of these positions questions
the truthfulness, the inspiration or the authority of the Bible.
Those who view *Jonah* as being more than a simple historical
narrative do so not because they question God's power, but
because they believe they see God's purpose and his original
intention in the book. Let us look at the question in more
detail.

If we ask the question, "Did Jonah actually live three days
and three nights in the belly of the fish," what kind of answers

128

will we get? Mr. A. will say, "No, it could not happen. Jonah would suffocate and be eaten up by the stomach acids." Mr. B. in turn will say, "But the Bible is the word of God and anything is possible with God. If you deny that Jonah lived three days and nights in the belly of the fish, then you deny the inspiration of the Bible." Mr. A. in turn replies, "I do not doubt the inspiration of the scripture. But, nevertheless, I believe the story of Jonah was told originally in the same way that the story of the Prodigal Son and the story of the Good Samaritan were told and that the Bible intended it this way. The story was told as a parable, and hence I in no way deny the inspiration of the scripture if I view it as a parable. I am merely being true to the original, God-inspired intention of the author."

"But the Bible does not say that *Jonah* is a parable," Mr. B. objects. "How can you claim that it is a parable?"

"Neither does the Bible say that the stories of the Good Samaritan and the Prodigal Son are parables," replies Mr. A. "Read these stories again (*Luke* 10:30-37 and 15:11-32). You do not doubt my belief in the inspiration of the scripture if I speak of the parable of the Good Samaritan. Why do you doubt my belief in the Bible if I speak of the parable of Jonah? The scriptural evidence for their being parables seems to be about the same. We have become so accustomed to speaking of the parable of the Good Samaritan that we overlook the fact that *Luke* 10:30-37 at no place says that the story is a parable. In response to the lawyer's question, 'Who is my neighbor?', Jesus tells a story. We assume that it was a parable. However, when Jesus begins by saying, 'A man was going down from Jerusalem to Jericho,' it could well be that he was relating an actual incident. Likewise *Luke* 15:11-32 does not say that the story of the Prodigal Son is a parable. Note that the story in *Luke* 15:3-7 (the Lost Sheep) is labeled a parable (verse 3). Also the story in 15:8-10 (the Lost Coin) is put in parabolic format. The introductory expression, 'or what woman . . .' indicates that the story is hypothetical. But in verse 11 the format changes. There is a simple 'historical' statement, 'There was a man who had two sons.' It is true that the man is not named. But there are many nameless persons in the Bible who are quite historical: the lawyer (*Luke* 10), the Samaritan woman (*John* 4), the man possessed with a demon (*Luke* 8) and many others. On what basis, then, do we call the story of the prodigal a parable, except that we have assumed that it falls into the same category as the two preceding stories? This is not necessarily the case. I am not attempting to argue that the Prodigal Son and the Good Samaritan were historical characters (though one today will be shown by tour guides the 'Good Samaritan Inn' on the road from Jerusalem to Jericho!). The point is that we in no way deny the inspiration of the Bible when we follow the commonly accepted orthodox procedure and call the stories parables. Whether or not the events or any part of the events actually happened, the stories are still told by Jesus as parables. The point which each makes is unmistakable. Therefore, in the same way, there is no reason to be disturbed if we speak of *Jonah* as a parable. The textual evidence for calling *Jonah* a parable seems to be rather similar to the textual evidence for calling the stories of the Good Samaritan and the Prodigal Son parables." [1]

Who is right—A or B? It can easily be seen that one's basic presuppositions will determine in large measure the answer he or she gives. If one has the scientific presuppositions of A, then A's arguments will be convincing. However, if one begins with the presuppositions of B, all of A's arguments will be rejected. A may go on to point out that there is no evidence whatever in Assyrian history that such a mass conversion as is spoken of in the book of *Jonah* ever took place in Nineveh. There is no evidence whatever that the Ninevites ever became Yahweh worshippers. Surely such a tremendous event, had it actually happened, would have been mentioned somewhere in Assyrian history. But as convincing as this argument may be, B can counter by pointing out that such an omission does not prove anything. There are many gaps in our knowledge of the past. In other words, the question turns out to be not one of the facts (which are the same for persons A and B) but of the personal context within which the person approaches the Bible. To point this out is not to minimize in any sense the importance of historical research; nor is it to indicate that the evidence on one side is as good as the evidence on the other. We are not at this point assessing the value of evidence. The purpose is only to suggest the fruitlessness of such arguments because of the fact that the value of evidence is assessed differently by different people.

The truth of this contention may be seen in the fact that there was a time only a few years ago when, under the complete sway of historical positivism, we were quite certain which reported events of the past could and which could not have happened. The simple formula was that anything that could not be explained in terms of our modern world view could not have actually happened, and was, therefore, an interpretation or a legend or a myth. Both those who denied and those who defended the historicity of *Jonah* accepted this historical positivism. Those who denied claimed that science made no place for the assumption that a man could stay alive three days and three nights in the belly of a fish. Those who defended were no less controlled by the same historical positivism as they set out to reconcile science with the Bible by attempting to show that a three-day visit in the belly of a fish is not a scientific impossibility. Elaborate efforts were made to find other incidents where fish had supposedly swallowed men whole. Pusey, for example, as noted in the exegesis on page 69, goes into elaborate detail describing different kinds of fish which are large enough to swallow a man, and reports a number of incidents where men or animals have allegedly been swallowed whole. In one case a sailor is supposed to have fallen overboard, have been swallowed, and later recovered alive. In another, a man is reported to have been taken from a fish near Marseilles "quite dressed and unhurt." [2]

Aside from the logical inconsistency that assumed that one event could prove another event in history, such parallels always turned out to be stories that were no more subject to proof than was the account they sought to prove—that is, the story of Jonah. Furthermore, the aim was totally misdirected because the entire procedure assumed that one had capitulated to historical positivism before he ever started. That is, the assumption underlying the entire enterprise was that that which can happen in the present and therefore is proven to be scientifically possible, is determinative for that which could and could not have happened in the past. It is the historical positivism itself that should have been attacked.

The attempt to find natural parallels to the events of *Jonah* actually downgrades the miraculous element in the book. It has the net effect of showing that the miracles were after all not real miracles, but natural occurrences. Thus the argument designed supposedly to defend faith turns out to be a denial of faith. If we read the book of *Jonah,* we will find that it is full of miracle. The entire emphasis is on God's action. Scientific possibility in terms of the modern world view is, therefore, not the point in question and only confuses the issue. God sent Jonah to Nineveh; God sent the storm on the sea; God prepared the fish to swallow Jonah; God caused the fish to vomit Jonah out; God had mercy on the Ninevites and saved them. God caused the vine to grow up in one day; God sent the worm to destroy the vine; God sent the sultry east wind; God rebuked Jonah. The book of *Jonah* speaks of God's action from beginning to end, and the attempt to find parallels or to prove the story scientifically misses the point entirely.

The appeal here is simply that we not be sidetracked onto a false issue and miss the meaning of *Jonah.* To argue the historicity of *Jonah* as though the book's authority as scripture depended on this is not only to be sidetracked onto a false issue, but is in effect to question the other non-historical portions of the Bible such as the parables, the psalms and the proverbs. Those who view *Jonah* as literal history will see the fish incident as a miracle and leave it at that. As already indicated, this is an entirely defensible faith position. However, those who believe that the story stands in the great Haggadic tradition will see it as a parable similar to those told by Jesus. (For another striking Old Testament parable see *II Samuel* 12: 1-7.) The weight of biblical scholarship in recent years favors this latter view because it opens up the rich meaning of the book. We wish to stress that both views affirm, and affirm clearly, that *Jonah* is authoritative scripture, the "word of God." Our plea here is that we accept the diversities of scriptural interpretation (which we surely must do if we respect Christians of denominations other than our own) and that, having done this, we proceed to the heart of the message of *Jonah.*

Footnotes

[1] I am aware that I am using the term *parable* here in a broad sense. Ordinarily, as stated above, the parable uses only fictitious characters. Yet, there is no inherent reason why an "expanded" parable (or sermon) could not employ historical characters.

[2] E. B. Pusey, *The Minor Prophets* (New York: Funk and Wagnalls, 1885), pp. 384-387.

ALLEGORY. A style of writing in which characters and events stand for or symbolize other persons, qualities, events or ideas. The characters and events, therefore, are not to be taken literally, but rather as symbols of something else. Through these characters and events one is to discover otherwise hidden meanings. A prime example of an allegory is John Bunyan's *Pilgrim's Progress*.

CANON. The *canon* like the word *cane* comes from the Greek word which means reed. The reed with its regular joints was used as a measuring instrument and hence the term came to mean a "rule" or "standard." The terms "Old Testament Canon" and "New Testament Canon" refer to the books accepted as authoritative scripture by the Christian church.

CENTRIFUGAL. To move outward away from a center or axis. A centrifugal force or movement is one which pulls outward away from the center.

CENTRIPETAL. To move inward toward a center or axis. A centripetal force or movement is one which pulls inward toward a center.

COMMUNITY. Community is used throughout this book in the sense of loving Christian fellowship and acceptance of persons as members of God's family.

COVENANT. An agreement between two parties. The covenant referred to in this book is the agreement entered into between Israel and Yahweh which we find discussed throughout the Old Testament.

EXEGESIS. Exegesis broadly speaking is biblical interpretation or the explanation of a passage of the Bible. The Greek verb from which the English "exegesis" is derived means literally "to lead out." The purpose of exegesis, then, is to "lead out," set forth, and explain what the biblical writer intended. It involves careful study of the historical context in which the passage was written as well as careful study of the text itself.

EXILE and EXILIC. The term *exile* refers to a period in Jewish history. In 586 B.C. the Babylonian Empire conquered the Kingdom of Judah and carried many of the Jewish people as captives to Babylon. In 538 B.C. Persia conquered Babylon and Cyrus, King of Persia, allowed the Jews to return to Jerusalem. The period 586-538 B.C. is spoken of as "The Exile."

EXISTENTIAL. The existence or personal experience of existence of the individual. It stresses subjective personal involvement in life, actual living in faith, in trust, in commitment, as over against objective and rationalistic contemplation of facts and concepts about life.

HEBREWS. The term *Hebrews* is used here as an equivalent for Israelites.

HUMANIZATION. The act or process of making human. We use the term here in a definitely Christian context in which Jesus Christ defines what it means to be human. This includes such concepts as love, justice, concern for others, community, and the development of full personhood.

INTERPOLATION. Used here to refer to an addition to or an insertion of words or phrases into the text.

ISRAELITES. The term *Israelites* refers to all the descendants of Jacob, who was re-named Israel (*Genesis* 32:28).

JEROBOAM II. King of the Northern Kingdom of Israel from 786-745 B.C.

LINGUA FRANCA. A common language spoken over a wide area by peoples of different ethnic backgrounds whose native languages are different.

MONOTHEISM. The belief in one God.

MONOTHEISTIC UNIVERSALISM. The belief that the one God who has created the entire universe has the same love and concern for all persons all over the world regardless of race, class or nationality. Those who believe in and worship God are required to manifest this universal love and concern for all persons.

NATIONALISTIC PARTICULARISM. The belief in the kind of uniqueness of one's national, ethnic, or religious group that demands a segregation of this group from other peoples. For the Jews it meant Jewish exclusivism.

PARABLE, PARABOLIC. The word *parable* comes from the Greek verb which means "to place beside" or "to compare." A parable may be a lengthy story or a brief simile. It places two realms of experience beside one another and compares them. It is not an illustration, but rather a lesson which is to be transferred from one realm of reality to another. The parables of Jesus are good examples. *Parabolic* is an adjective, meaning that something is told in the form of a parable.

PIOUS, PIETY. These terms refer to the quality or state of being devoted to one's religious beliefs. The term at times may carry objectionable connotations (as when one is overly pious) but here it is used simply to refer to one's loyalty to one's religious convictions.

POLYTHEISM. The belief in many gods.

POST-EXILIC. The period after the Exile—after 538 B.C. (See Exile above).

PRE-EXILIC. The period before the Exile—before 586 B.C.

PREJUDICE. Means literally "prejudging" or forming an opinion before one knows all the facts. In this book it carries the connotation of an irrational attitude of hostility directed against an individual or a group such as an ethnic group or a racial group.

PREVENIENT GRACE. The doctrine that God's grace precedes (pre: before; venio: come) any action on a person's part to repent or move toward God. Apart from this grace the person is helpless to repent and to move toward God.

PROPHET, PROPHECY, PROPHETIC. In the Old Testament a prophet is one who speaks for God. Prophecy is that which is spoken by the prophet as the word of God. Prophetic is the adjective which describes the spoken or written word.

SECOND ISAIAH OR DEUTERO ISAIAH. Refers to Isaiah 40-66. Almost all Old Testament scholars agree that Isaiah 1-39, called I Isaiah, is by one author and 40-66, called II Isaiah or Deutero Isaiah, is by another.

SEPTUAGINT. The Greek translation of the Hebrew Old Testament made around 200 B.C.

SOLA FIDE. Salvation by faith alone (Fide: faith; Sola: alone).

STATUS QUO. Refers to the present conditions that prevail and carries the connotation of remaining static, of keeping things as they are.

TECHNETRONIC. A combination of technology and electronics. The term applies to our society which increasingly is shaped culturally, psychologically, socially and economically by technology and electronics.

UNIVERSALISM. Used in the ordinary sense of "world wide," and has no reference to the theological doctrine of "universal salvation."

WORD, WORD OF THE LORD. These terms refer to God's "speaking" or his disclosure of his will. See Exegesis, pp. 19-20.

YAHWEH. Hebrew name for God. See footnote 23, p. 22 for an explanation of this term.

BIBLIOGRAPHY

Books

Bewer, Julius, *A Critical And Exegetical Commentary on Haggai, Zechariah, Malachi and Jonah*. New York: Charles Scribner's Sons, 1912. One of the volumes of the *International Critical Commentary*, ed., Briggs, Charles A., et al.

Bowman, Locke E., Jr., et al., *National Teacher Education Project Manual*. The Arizona Experiment, 6947 East MacDonald Dr., Scottsdale, Arizona, 1970.

Bull, G. T. *The City and the Sign: An Interpretation of the Book of Jonah*. New York: Baker Books, 1972.

Burrows, M. "The Literary Category of the Book of Jonah," in *Translating and Understanding the Old Testament*. Ed. by H. T. Frank and W. L. Reed. Nashville: Abingdon Press, 1970. (See pages 80-107.)

Carlisle, Thomas John. *You! Jonah!* Grand Rapids, Michigan: Wm. B. Eerdmans, 1971.

Carothers, J. Edward. *Keepers of the Poor*. New York: Board of Missions of the Methodist Church, 1966.

Carothers, J. Edward. *The Church and Cruelty Systems*. New York: Friendship Press, 1970.

Castel, Helene, ed. *World Development: An Introductory Reader*. New York: The Macmillan Co., 1971.

Corbett, J. Elliott. *The Prophets on Main Street*. Richmond, Virginia: John Knox Press, 1966.

Driver, S. R. *An Introduction to the Literature of the Old Testament*. New York: Charles Scribner's Sons, 1903.

Eiselen, Frederick Carl. *The Minor Prophets*. New York: Eaton and Mains, 1907.

Ellul, Jacques. *The Judgment of Jonah*. Grand Rapids, Michigan: Wm. B. Eerdmans, 1971.

Faramelli, Norman J. *Technethics*. New York: Friendship Press, 1971.

Funk, Robert. *Language, Hermeneutic and Word of God*. New York: Harper and Row, 1966.

Gottwald, Norman K. *A Light to the Nations*. New York: Harper and Brothers, 1959.

Harrell, Costen J. *The Prophets of Israel*. Nashville: Cokesbury Press, 1923.

Harmon, Nolan B., editor. *The Interpreter's Bible*. Vol. VI. Nashville: Abingdon Press, 1956. (See page 880.)

Henshaw, T. *The Latter Prophets*. London: George Allen and Unwin, Ltd., 1958.

Horton, R. F. *The Minor Prophets*. 2 vols. New York: Henry Froude, n.d.

Kennedy, James Hardee. *Studies in the Book of Jonah*. Nashville: Broadman Press, 1956.

Kent, Charles Foster. *The Sermons, Epistles and Apocalypses of Israel's Prophets*. New York: Charles Scribner's Sons, 1910.

Knight, George A. F. *Ruth and Jonah*. London: S. C. M. Press, 1960.

Kuhn, Margaret E. *Get Out There and Do Something About Injustice*. New York: Friendship Press, 1972.

Little, Sara. *Learning Together in the Christian Fellowship*. Richmond: John Knox Press, 1958.

Mankowitz, Wolf. "It Should Happen to a Dog," *Religious Drama 3*, selected and introduced by Marvin Halverson. New York: Meridian Books, The World Publishing Co., 1959.

Minor, Harold D., editor. *Techniques and Resources for Guiding Adult Groups*. Nashville: Abingdon Press, 1972.

Morris, Colin. *Include Me Out*. Nashville: Abingdon Press, 1968.

Morris, Colin. *Unyoung, Uncolored, Unpoor*. Nashville: Abingdon Press, 1969.

Munby, Denys. *World Development: A Challenge to the Churches*. Cleveland: Corpus Books, 1969.

Myers, Jacob M. *Hosea to Jonah*. London: S. C. M. Press, 1959.

Napier, B. Davie. *Time of Burning*. Philadelphia: Pilgrim Press, 1970.

Paterson, John. *The Goodly Fellowship of the Prophets*. New York: Charles Scribner's Sons, 1948.

Phillips, J. B. *Your God Is Too Small*. London: Epworth Press, 1962.

Smith, George Adam. *The Book of the Twelve Prophets*. New York: Charles Scribner's Sons, 1948.

Smith, J. M. Powis. *The Prophets and Their Times*. Chicago: The University of Chicago Press, 1925.

Ward, Barbara. *The Lopsided World*. New York: W. W. Norton, 1968.

Ward, Barbara. *The Rich Nations and the Poor Nations*. New York: W. W. Norton, 1962.

Weber, Hans Ruedi. *The Invitation*. New York: Joint Commission on Education and Cultivation of the Board of Missions, The United Methodist Church, 1971.

Wright, Elliott. *Go Free*. New York: Friendship Press, 1973.

Articles

Childs, B. "Jonah: A Study in Old Testament Hermeneutics" in *Scottish Journal of Theology II*, 1958.

Cohen, A. "The Tragedy of Jonah" in *Judaism 82*, 1972.

Landes, George M. "The Kerygma of the Book of Jonah: The Contextual Interpretation of the Jonah Psalm" in *Interpretation 21*, 1967.

Landes, George M. "The Three Days and Three Nights Motif in Jonah 2:1" in *Journal of Biblical Literature*, 1967.

Lewis, C. "Jonah—A Parable for Our Time" in *Judaism 82*, 1972.

Audiovisual

"Jonah, the Reluctant Missionary," 55 frames. $10 filmstrip with record, $7 filmstrip with script only. Produced by Cathedral Films and Filmstrips, 2921 W. Alameda Ave., Box 1608, Burbank, California 91505.

THE AUTHOR

William M. Pickard is chairman of the Religion and Philosophy Department at Huntingdon College, Montgomery, Alabama. He is an ordained minister, a member of the Alabama-West Florida Annual Conference of The United Methodist Church. Born in Alabama and reared in a Methodist parsonage, he is a Phi Beta Kappa graduate of Randolph Macon College, Ashland, Virginia, and holds the B.D. and Ph.D. degrees from Emory University in Atlanta, Georgia. From 1954 to 1970 he served as a missionary of The United Methodist Church in the Philippines, first as a rural district missionary in northern Luzon, then as pastor of the 4,500 member Knox Memorial United Methodist Church in Manila, and later as professor in the Union Theological Seminary in Manila. In 1970 he served the Board of Global Ministries of The United Methodist Church as Acting Executive Secretary for work in Hong Kong, Taiwan, Philippines and the South Pacific. Not able to return to the Philippines in 1971, he accepted his present position at Huntingdon College.

The author is married to the former Mary Ann Martin of Decatur, Georgia, a graduate of Agnes Scott College. They have five children. Desiring to continue in mission and to keep their roots deep in the local church, the Pickards on coming to Montgomery requested the bishop to assign them to a small rural church in addition to the duties at the college. Dr. and Mrs. Pickard serve as a team in the pastoral ministry at the Woodland United Methodist Church, twelve miles east of Montgomery, where they reside in the parsonage with their two youngest children, Earl and Paul. Their daughter, Susan, married in August 1973 and lives in Atlanta, Georgia. Henry, the oldest son, is in graduate school at the University of Virginia (Astro-Physics) and Marshall, the second son, is in college at Huntingdon.

Prepared by the Education and Cultivation Division
Board of Global Ministries • The United Methodist Church

SERVICE CENTER

7820 Reading Road • Cincinnati, Ohio 45237

JBW/2-74—Price $1.45